OBAMA
v.
ROMNEY
Taxes and the Economy!

By: NICHOLAS PALEVEDA MBA J.D. LL.M,
Adjunct Professor, Graduate Tax Program, Northeastern University, Boston.

ISBN 13:978-1478113621
ISBN 10:1478113626

"The salvation of this human world lies nowhere else than in the human heart, in the human power to reflect, in human meekness and human responsibility."

Václav Hável as quoted
In the International
Herald Tribune (Paris)

Table of Contents

YOUR TAXES

Unfortunately, in politics, much of what we hear and see is a mixture of fact and fiction. Even with tax policy, the misinformation is swirling. Still, taxes are really quantitative issues that need to be considered independently of other issues, especially race, religion, and politics. Obama got it right when he said, "There is no blue America or red America, there is no black America or white America--there is The United States of America." Tax policy affects each of us differently. The tax policies put forward by each candidate are almost opposite in how they affect each segment of taxpayers. The choice in this election will determine our ability to meet our obligations.

We need to choose wisely.

Tax Cuts -- Who Saves You More?
Or, Who Costs You More?

If your income is:		Obama		Romney
Less than $19,000		$567.00		$19.00
$38,000 to $66,000		$892.00		$113.00
$112,000 to $161,000		$2,204.00		$2,614.00
$227,000 to $603,000	Increase	$12.00	Decrease	$7,871.00
$2.9 million plus	Increase	$701,885.00	Decrease	$269,364.00

Unless an increase is indicated, all amounts are tax savings.

In addition, Obama proposes a "Make Work Pay" refundable income tax credit of 6.2% on the first $8,100 earned. In this way, the Social Security revenue stream is maintained, but ten million low-income workers would have their income tax eliminated. The credit is up to $500 for a single person, and $1,000 for a family. In this way, the Social Security revenue stream is maintained, but ten million low income workers would have their income tax eliminated.

Obama v. Republican Tax Plans

IRS CIRCULAR 230 STANDARDS

The new rules require us to add certain standard language to any correspondence regarding federal tax matters unless we are willing to undertake extensive analysis of the facts underlying a transaction and legal authority that address the tax treatment of the transaction.

IRS REGULATION REQUIRE US TO ADVISE YOU THAT, UNLESS OTHERWISE SPECIFICALLY NOTED, ANY FEDERAL TAX ADVICE IN THIS COMMUNICATION (INCLUDING ANY ATTACHMENTS, ENCLOSURES, OR ACCOMPANYING MATERIALS) WAS NOT INTENDED OR WRITTEN TO BE USED, AND IT CANNOT BE USED, BY ANY TAXPAYER FOR THE PURPOSE OF AVOIDING PENALTIES; FUTHERMORE, THIS COMMUNICATION WAS NOT INTENDED OR WRITTEN TO SUPPORT THE PROMOTION OR MARKETING OF ANY OR THE TRANSACTIONS OR MATTERS IT ADDRESSES.

The new rules require such notice to be "prominently disclosed" and "readily apparent to the reader. The notice must be in a separate section (but not in a footnote or as fine print) of the correspondence. The typeface used must be at least the same size as the typeface used in any discussions of facts or law.

This new rule was put into place after the many abuses on tax matters occurred with major CPA firms and major law firms participating. I have a collection of several of these "tax opinion letters" written when Circular 230 did not have any teeth or any disciplinary actions attached to standards of tax practice. Many of these firms are well known law firms with stellar reputations who of course would deny any wrong doing as they participated in tax shelter opinions prior to the teeth being placed in Circular 230.

This book is written on and about the tax policies of two current presidential candidates. The views expressed are opinions only and can vary as no final bill has been passed nor has one even been submitted to Congress for review.

AMERICAN BAR ASSOCIATION
DECLARATION

FOREWORD

This book is designed to be fun, entertaining and thought provoking. If you feel uncomfortable at any point, keep going. Either the next section will reduce your discomfort, or you really need to keep reading. All the errors contained in the book are the fault of the editor and staff; the writer takes no responsibility whatsoever. You are encouraged to read this book at your own risk. The book has not been approved or disapproved by the Federal Elections Commission or the FDA, and contains material which may not be suitable for all audiences and is not rated by the Motion Picture Association. The facts are subject to change without notice. Any perceived opinions are misunderstood facts. This book is also designed to confuse bibliophiles and librarians. Should it be classified under fiction or non-fiction, humor or history, business or current events? Remember Americans like their "branding" and "labels"; and this book transcends many of them which will make it difficult to settle on the proper placement of this book in the store, or library. Hopefully at the end, you will have no idea as to the candidate we support.

This book is not about us. This book is about you and your vision for America.

If you are a pinko commie hippie freak who would vote the Democratic ticket if Chairman Mao was running with Lenin, this book is not for you. If you are a gun toting, bible thumping right wing freak who would vote for the Republican ticket if Hoover was running with Calvin Coolidge, this book is not for you.

However, if you are an independent thinker who is a member of either party, or an independent, or just plain fed up and convinced that they all lie, yet concerned about how the election will affect you directly; this book is for you. This book will give you an indication as to how much this election will cost or save you over the next four years. The tax and economic policies of each candidate are radically different; and the choice you make will have a direct and indirect affect on what you can buy, what you can save, where you can go, how long you can stay there and so forth. More important, this election will determine the direction of this country more than any election since the election of Franklin D. Roosevelt in 1936. This is probably because the situation we are in right now is as much as a crisis as the Great Depression.

The economy is in a period of a transition into a world economy. Unfortunately, the policies of the present administration have put the country in a position where the deficits have almost eliminated options usually available in a time of momentous and potentially catastrophic transition. David Walker, the former Comptroller General of the United States, authored, "A Call to Stewardship" with the Government Accountability Office. In 1797, the federal budget represented 2 percent of the national economy. Today it represents more than 20 percent. There are many factors contributing to this growth, not the least being the tendency to continue programs and agencies long after their missions have been completed. We need to completely overhaul the government and retain only the programs that are needed. "Without meaningful action, by 2040, our government could only have resources to do little more than mail out Social Security checks and pay interest on the massive and growing national debt. This is obviously an unacceptable scenario."

> "Our current long-range fiscal path is clearly imprudent and fiscally unsustainable. It is also alarming given the range of current and emerging problems that require attention: health care, energy dependency, environmental protection, and homeland security, to name a few. These long-term challenges have profound implications for our future economic growth, standard of living, and national security. . . .What is needed is a more strategic, long-term, comprehensive, and integrated approach to help capitalize on related opportunities and manage related risks within current and expected resource levels." Introductory Letter Page iv.

Mr. Walker resigned in March of this year. He had embarked on a vigorous "Fiscal Wake-Up Tour", which was not supported by the Administration because it clearly described the looming monetary crisis facing the nation. Worse yet, poor fiscal management has been compounded by failure to address energy and trade policies. The result is seen in an increasingly strapped middle class. The black community has been particularly compromised by the drug laws. The K-12 education system is in crisis, higher education faces serious challenges; the military is severely overextended, and immigration has become a threat to both national security, and domestic stability; the health care system is in crisis; and no one wants to address the dimension and scope of the challenges we face with clear sighted honesty. Actually, I can't blame them. I wish I didn't have to.

Tax policy and our approach to economic policy dwarf the impact of any other element in the success or failure of resolving these existential issues. For too long, we have allowed the issues of gay rights and abortion to hold hostage meaningful discussions about how to address the massive challenges growing larger every day. These issues are religious issues that really don't belong in the conversation at all. They are matters of conscience and personal choice. The issues are complicated. Since we have been arguing these issues for almost 50 years with no resolution in sight, perhaps we need to set them aside for a time, let emotions cool, and go back to them when we are willing to listen to one another. We have issues facing us that may eliminate our ability to decide these issues for ourselves, because we may no longer be in control of our national destiny.

The book covers only tax and economic policy because the writers have expertise in this area. We do not cover any of what we believe are the "red herring" issues—such as energy, the war in Iraq, gay rights, abortion, environmental policies, etc.—which are meant to distract the reader from the impact of economic policy both on personal well-being and moral obligation to their neighbors.

Tax policy determines more than the amount of revenue raised. Tax policy reflects the values of the electorate, the collective goals of individual taxpayers. The most critical impact of tax policy is the influence on taxpayer behavior. As we shall see, the dramatically lower marginal tax rates on higher levels of income seems to have resulted in runaway executive compensation, and contributed to the loss of American jobs to foreign countries. The media sources have slowly consolidated under the umbrella of fewer and fewer, larger and larger corporate conglomerates holding increasing control over the topics reported and the way the news is presented.

News has been reduced to entertainment; and the media are controlled by fewer and fewer sources each day. You have to LOOK for facts. Most of the TV and news sources are completely controlled by the corporate entities that own them. For example, on August 31, Pickensplan.org sent out an email requesting that supporters contact NBC. Why? Seems NBC had refused to run a 15 second ad announcing that IRAN was switching every automobile in the country to natural gas, so that they could sell ALL their oil to us at $120 per gallon. Wake up America. In this country, the State of Utah has worked with private industry to create a statewide chain of LNG stations. People there are buying kits to change their cars over to LNG selling for **87 CENTS per gallon.** Why would NBC not run this ad? Perhaps this is not in the best interests of GE, their parent company. Perhaps the powers that be are supporting The republicans and Big Oil. Whatever the reason, this demonstrates how freedom of the press is now bought and paid for.

Many of the newspaper ads, television promotions and "news programs" are meant to mislead. Commentators are paid to "stay on message". In too many cases, any relationship between their personal beliefs and the views they present does not exist. Lou Dobbs, Jim Lehrer, Anderson Cooper and Christiane Amanpour come immediately to mind as having both feet planted in reality, most of the time. Larry King is notable for his ability to demonstrate complete absence of an agenda with every interview. That absence of an agenda is why we watch him. I wish the same could be said for his guests. The political guests, in particular, often are too busy staying on message and using the labels most calculated to remove any possible light of truth and replace truth with an emotional derogatory barb. The result is that any hope of a meaningful discussion is eliminated.

YOU HAVE A DUTY TO GO TO OTHER SOURCES THAN THE ONES YOU ALWAYS USE, AND LEARN THE FACTS.

We have listed sources we consider reliable in the appendix. Verify the information through another source with an alternate agenda. Also, remember there is a distinction between outright untruths and simplification. Don't argue details when the essential facts are truthful. Keep in mind that most of the time, even when you are diligent in seeking the truth, you only get part of it. Step out of your comfort zone and try the other side. Most of all, remember that the past does not dictate the future and is often irrelevant to the solution of a current problem. As Einstein observed, (this is approximate) you will not get out of the current mess at the same level of thinking that got you into it. We need to find the way out, and that will require that we learn and grow.

There is a second, more insidious problem facing news-craving Americans today: variety. While we may pride ourselves on the number of news sources we read each day, it is critical to remember that number is not the same as variety. When faced with a large number of news options, we tend to choose sources that already match our own beliefs. We can actually be more narrow-minded than someone who only has 2 sources. Knowing this, we can choose to step outside of our usual news-circle, and then we face a different obstacle: confirmation bias. Confirmation bias is something that everyone has. It's part of how our brains work. When we receive new information, our brain strives to fits the new information into what we already 'know'. This is very useful in a lot of areas, but it can also get us into trouble. For example, if you were to tell a tree-hugging pot-smoking hippie that 60% of all arrests in his town stemmed from possession of marijuana, he might think "What a shame that we waste all that money and time arresting harmless pot-smokers. We should just legalize it, man." And if you give the same statistic to an SUV-driving, Bible-thumping, NRA lifer, he might tell you that we should: "Slap the death penalty on all those drug-peddling scum."

Media corporations rely on these two facts in order to maintain their revenue stream, namely, you. They have 5 different ways to tell you the same thing, and then they over-simplify the issue until it fits into whatever view you already hold.

But, you might ask, what impact can the President REALLY have on economic policy? I thought he was just a figurehead!

Taxes and the National Debt affect EVERY American in EVERYDAY life, and the President of the United States has a great influence both on taxes and on the economy. The President of the United States gets universal media coverage every time he speaks; so, he controls what issues get discussed and how they are presented. This in and of itself is influential enough but let's remember the power of the veto, the Executive Exception (in effect this is a veto), and the Executive Order (can "override" the law). Even more effective, he can threaten to veto legislation. This is why we MUST use facts and figures to evaluate candidates, not feelings.

Each candidate will have a web site that summarizes, in plain English the programs of each candidate. That is where we got our information on what these policies are.

Also, prayer is not really useful in this arena. There are about equal numbers of prayerful people voting for each of the candidates. In our house the rule is if the two of us don't get the same answer, the answer is, "No". I think decisions on who to vote for deserve more work and less prayer. Also, separation of church and state might **not** deny the Ten Commandments on school walls, but it must certainly deny the application of religious beliefs to determine, not influence, but determine, laws. Religious beliefs are matters of intensely personal choice. We are a Democracy; not a Theocracy. (Iran is a theocracy.) If you don't think that the road to governmental hell is paved by passing religion-based laws, I have a bridge to sell you . . .

Finally, in closing, we wrote this book because we love this crazy country. We love its faults, we love its energy. We love our compassion for the less fortunate, and our amazing creativity. We love that when we wake up every morning, we have the right to go out there and make complete idiots of ourselves in the pursuit of noble, mundane, wrong-headed, constructive, destructive, unwise, reckless, selfish, generous, small, or huge goals and whatever else we choose. We love those who have gone before to pave the way for us to enjoy our freedoms, our prosperity, our dreams, our families. WE OWE THEM. We honor them when we do our best and are the best that we can be. We need to demonstrate our love for them by loving this country enough to admit we have been wrong and take responsibility to face the challenges ahead with courage, integrity and the determination to leave our children a legacy of love, of obligations met, and of a better world.

Inspiration!

Thanks to my cousin, the late William Saxbe, United States Attorney General under Richard Nixon, and Gerald Ford who inspired me to go to law school, thanks to Roy Black, my law professor at the University of Miami, Stuart Miller, my classmate at the University of Miami who was a great student, and is now the CEO of Lennar Corporation. He donated $100 million to the University of Miami Medical School.

We owe a special word of thanks to Jerome Corsi PhD (Harvard!) for writing the book "ObamaNation". If that book can make it to the top of **The New York Times** bestseller list, then even this book has a shot! He was the primary motivator to write this book at first. In the process of writing it, we discovered that we needed to write this book and that we would publish it - whatever the cost. We also discovered that, try as we might, any objective examination of the facts eliminated our ability to remain neutral.

"The great enemy of the truth is very often not the lie-
deliberate, contrived and dishonest-

but the myth-
persistent, persuasive and unrealistic."

JFK (New Haven) 1962

THE TWO PLANS – AN OVERVIEW

Now, Barack Obama has provided a relatively detailed policy report on his proposed changes. You will note that his provisions contain many elements designed to relieve the middle class of some of the burden. He has provisions to expand the Earned Income Credit, provide a Universal Mortgage Credit of 10% of mortgage interests for those who do not itemize up to $800. This means that homeowners receive a 10% credit on the first $8,000 of mortgage interest. This means that even homeowners in the most expensive markets will have a little relief. There will be a new buyers' credit for first-time farm owners. He has a well thought-out farm proposal. His proposal includes a Small Business and Microenterprise credit of 20% for the first $50,000 of investment in a small owner-operated business.

Most important to seniors, he includes a provision that seniors making less than $50,000 per year will have no income tax. At least one of the candidates is aware that most people in their late fifties and early sixties realize that they will be working into their seventies. They simply have not been able to save enough. Why? The wages for most people have stagnated since 1980. We see the employer censuses for many small businesses. Typically the compensation for most employees is between $20,000 and $40,000. At today's price levels, they can't afford health insurance, they are driving old used cars, and they see their movies at home using one of the rental sources. Employers actually expect them to contribute to the company 401(k). My question is always, "With what?'

As a small business owner, those tax cuts will help my employees and help my business. Raising the highest marginal income tax rates on the top wage earners will increase the incentive for employers to establish and generously contribute to employee retirement plans. Even a small increase in the top marginal rate will help slow the loss of jobs to overseas operations because for every percentage you raise the highest marginal tax rate; there is a reduced incentive for executives to give themselves exorbitant salaries. That is what kept executive compensation from ballooning out of control until 1980.

In contrast, The republicans allows all businesses to expense (deduct in one year) short-term assets purchased for the business. Basically, he just makes the current Section 179 deduction permanent. Make no mistake; this will help some small businesses. The problem is that for many of us the significant equipment purchases occur in the first five years of the business. Those first five years are not generally very profitable. If they are, you have a great problem. For most small businesses expensing equipment is less of a benefit than for large corporations. The reason is quite simple. Large corporations spend enormous sums on equipment. Once again, Corporate America will benefit in real terms more than

Small Business America.

Romney reduces the maximum corporate tax rate to 25% from 35%. This will have the effect of encouraging corporations, reduce their contributions to retirement plans, depress wages for the rank and file, and ship more jobs overseas. Thanks, John. He will increase the personal exemption for everyone by 70%. What will this do? Well if you are making $250,000 and the personal exemption is increased, for every dollar you deduct from your gross income, your benefit will be 35 cents. If you are below the lowest marginal rate, you won't benefit at all. Those in the middle will benefit less than 35 cents. Get it?

And here is a good one. He will suspend the federal gas tax from Memorial Day to Labor Day. Good. He is keeping us hooked on foreign oil. What about a credit for kits to convert to Liquefied Natural Gas (LNG), or a credit for using mass transportation or for wind mill investment? At least then we would be moving away from oil.

His help for business is to make the R & D credit into a 10% credit for compensation paid for R & D development. In contrast, Obama provides that the R & D credit AND the renewable energy *production* credit (wind, solar) be made permanent.

For small businesses the republicans will tax employees on the value of employer provided health insurance to then provide a $5,000 credit towards the purchase of individual coverage. This means that the rank and file will be taxed for the first time in national history to fund a $5,000 credit for EVERY family in America. Are you listening Warren Buffet, Bill Gates, Paul Allen, Paris Hilton? Now he wants the least among us to finance the wealthiest among us in securing health care. How Republican. Further, the $5,000 credit will not come close to the $12,000 to $14,000 cost of individual policies. The republicans has promised cheaper drugs and lower health care costs. However, the American Medical Association has been very successful at restricting the number of doctors graduating from medical schools and the number of hospitals to serve their internships and residency training. Until we increase the number of medical schools and increase the number of students graduating from medical school each year, health care costs will be held hostage to the doctors. Both candidates offer programs to increase the use of technology and access to care.

Obama also has a comprehensive agenda for health care. He would:
- Provide a 50% credit for premiums paid for employee health insurance by small business owners. This is a great help to them.
- Subsidies for the cost of insurance for those who need it.
- Make the same insurance coverage provided for Senators available to everyone

14

- Create a national pool so that small businesses would enjoy the same benefit of spreading risk among a larger group that large businesses enjoy
- Reduce volatility by reimbursing premiums for catastrophic coverage
- Work to bring health care costs under control and place more emphasis on preventive care.

The difference between the two plans is significant. The republicans is once again both leaving people "on their own", and increasing the cost of health care for both business owners and their employees. Now every "conservative" web site and pundit spins the difference as being that the republicans tax cuts will stimulate business growth while Obama's plan is a "redistribution" plan. This makes no sense. As we saw in Chart 1, the lower taxes simply resulted in greater concentration of income for the top one percent. The economy has been in a free fall for the past two years, despite the generous Bush II tax cuts already in place. Please sell the Republican faithful on this "Bridge to Nowhere". And by the way, Sarah Palin supported that bridge before she was against it, after it became a national embarrassment.

Obama wants a tax credit for alternative energy production and will provide federal money to support investment in alternative energy. He includes provisions to give small and micro-businesses access to capital. His proposals will stimulate the development of new green industries, and bring new jobs that cannot be shipped overseas. The republicans would pursue drilling for oil which does nothing to address dependence on oil, nothing to support the development of green energy sources, and keep the middle class supporting the transfer of assets and income to the wealthy. Obama's goal is to stimulate the growth of new businesses with good high-paying jobs and provide relief to the lower-income and middle class.

With respect to the capital gains tax, Obama will increase maximum capital gains rate to 20%. This is a start. Remember the country prospered with the rate at 28%. Actually, the country prospered when the holding period was 2 years and the tax rate on capital gains was 50%. Obama will require documentation for reporting the basis used to compute any gains. The basis is the amount you paid for the asset, generally. He will eliminate capital gains taxation for start-up businesses and provide capital gains tax breaks for landowners selling to beginning family farmers. The republicans will keep the current tax rates on capital gains and dividend interest. This is a huge benefit to the top 5% in taxable income. We have already alluded to the downside of this policy. When the deficits are as huge as those we face right now--Social Security payments are going to swamp this country relatively soon--we have to rethink our tax system, at least in the short term. Once again, Barack Obama actually has policies to help small business, family farms, and the middle class. The republican's policies favor the wealthiest among us.

The Bush Tax Cuts are addressed quite differently by the two candidates. Barack Obama would keep the provisions most helpful to middle class families and repeal the provisions favoring the wealthy. The republicans would make the Bush tax cuts permanent, except for the capital gains tax. Obama would keep the marriage penalty relief, expand the adoption credit, the marginal tax rates would be 10%, 15%, 25%, and 28% and expand the Earned Income Tax Credit. He would restore the 36% and 39.6% marginal rates on higher income earners. This would return us to a situation closer to the situation during the Clinton administration when there was real economic growth for most of us.

The positions on the Estate Tax are most interesting. Now keep in mind that the republicans inherited a company worth in excess of $100,000,000. Unfortunately, her half sister inherited $10,000, and the republicans canceled her father's promise to pay for graduate school for her nephew. Then consider the compounding effect of wealth. Now as we will observe in the "conversations" with the candidates, the more you have, the more you get.

- If you double $50,000 you get $100,000
- If you double $100,000, you get $200,000
- If you double $1,000,000, you get $2,000,000
- If you double $10,000,000, you get $20,000,000
- If you double $100,000,000, you get $200,000,000

Can you see where wealthy people will not suffer from increased taxes? Can you understand how difficult it is for ordinary middle class people to get ahead? Do you really think we need to repeal the Estate Tax? Why has the wealth gap widened exponentially since 1980? The Reagan/Bush/Romney tax policies have done the opposite of what was promised. We are not better off. We are in terrible trouble. Bill Clinton raised the highest marginal rate, and the economy grew, and everyone shared in the growth. In contrast, under Bush II, the top one percent have prospered.

Both would extend the stop-gap Alternative Minimum Tax and then index it to inflation so that the tax would not weigh so heavily on middle income taxpayers. The republicans would also further increase the exemption by 5% above inflation after 2013. (Temporarily) The republicans favors repeal of the tax.

Both candidates will eliminate oil and gas tax loopholes. The republicans will somehow broaden the corporate tax base; eliminate earmarks from budget, freeze non-military discretionary spending for one year, and cut "wasteful" programs. During the moratorium on increases to discretionary spending, the administration will evaluate all federal agencies to streamline operations, cut ineffective programs, and reduce waste.

Obama will raise revenue to offset his tax cuts and programs by:

- Closing loopholes for the deductibility of CEO executive compensation
- Taxing carried interest as ordinary income, and increase the highest bracket for capital gains
- Reforming multinational tax deductions
- Making the economic substance doctrine law to eliminate manipulation of transactions
- Creating closer monitoring of "tax haven" countries to ensure that citizens pay their share of taxes regardless of domicile, and put uncooperative countries on a "watch list"
- Miscellaneous other provisions

It would appear that Obama is far less rigid and far more willing to spread tax increases over more of the tax base than The republicans.

That summarizes the major provisions of the competing tax policies. The republican's energy program offers very little in the way of lateral thinking or creativity, Obama puts many alternatives on the table.

IF YOU EARN LESS THAN $100,000 A YEAR, YOU SHOULD VOTE FOR OBAMA-HERE IS THE BREAKDOWN.

The Obama Tax Plan

The tax plan for Mr. Obama is quite clear, the rich would pay more and the poor and middle class would pay less. Under The republican plan, the rich would pay much, much less than they do now; and the poor and middle class would pay just a little less. The federal deficit would grow.

For the last eight years, the United States has adopted a policy that lowers the tax rates for individuals who are in the top 1% who received tax benefits averaging about $55,000. The low income individuals received about a $70 savings. The Tax Policy Center created a study that demonstrates the result of both proposals. Under Obama, the higher income individual would pay more in taxes while the lower income person's tax bill would be reduced. Under The republicans, high income individuals would benefit more than anyone else.

Under both plans, all Americans would pay a price for their tax cuts due to a bigger deficit. Under John Romney's plan, the national debt would grow by $4.5 trillion over the next ten years. Under Obama, the national debt would grow by $3.3 trillion. Neither plan would raise enough funds to cover government cost over the next ten years. How would the tax policy impact you?

Americans earning less than $19,000 per year

If you are in this category, chances are you did not buy this book because you cannot afford to buy this book.

The republicans plan to lower your taxes-that is great! Republicans are wonderful! Tax savings for me! Yes you save $19 a year, isn't that wonderful. Look what you could do with the $19. You could go out to Mc Donald's about 4 times, pay for a half of tank of gas, pay part of an overdraft charge on your credit card if you have one. Pay part of a service fee for an overdraft of a bank check. Life is good! You may even be able to afford this book once it is out in paperback and the election is over.

With Barack Obama's plan--you would save $567. Not much, but you could pay down some of the credit cards; you could pay one month's rent on a small apartment. You could even afford to buy this book and have money left over! You could pay down some of those credit cards, or perhaps if the debts are paid, use funds to purchase a new TV or even save money in a 401(k) that will be matched by your employer and now you have over $1,000 in your retirement account.

Americans earning between $19,000 and $38,000

Under the republicans plan you would receive back $113. This would be enough to buy this book, pay down some credit cards, fill up the gas tank twice and life is good.
Under the Obama plan, you would save $892. What could you do with these funds? Perhaps pay a month's worth of rent or maybe two months. Pay off credit card debt. Pay down car loans.

Americans earning between $38,000 and $66,000

This is Middle America. The average working person earns about $45,000 per year. Most Americans will fall in this category. What would the tax plan look like to you?
With the republicans you would save $319. What could you do with all this

money? Pay down credit card debt which averages about $8,000. Pay down your mortgage which averages about $81,000 (before the subprime mess). It will not pay rent on an average apartment for even one month.

Under Obama's plan you would save $1,042. You could use this to pay one month's rent, pay down credit card debt-and reduce your credit card debt each year with this savings. In 4 years, you would be down to $4,000 in debt. If the Obama plan continues, you would be debt free at the end of his 8 year administration.

Middle Income between $66,000 and $100,000

You will save approximately $1,009 with John Romney and $1,290 with Barack Obama. The savings can vary based upon the final Act which is passed by Congress and signed into law and is subject to change without notice. Read my lips, "No new taxes". Remember, these are promises made by politicians-see your tax advisor for details.

IF YOU ARE EARNING BETWEEN $100,000 and $250,000

Americans earning between $100,000 and $161,000

This group has purchasing power and in many cases consists of stressed out two income families. There is not much left over after the house mortgage, children's education, car payments etc. This is also where Romney and Obama's plan start to favor The republicans. Under the republican plan, the taxpayer would save about $2,614. Under Obama's plan; the taxpayer would save about $2,204. Romney would be the favored candidate of this group. This group is where American's will need to look at other issues as the tax benefits are roughly the same. As you approach $161,000 in income, the republican plan will start to benefit you more than Obama. When you earn less, the Obama plan would be in your best interest. Other factors should now come into play such as Foreign Policy, Domestic policy, the U.S. Debt etc.

Most of these issues are beyond the scope of this text. With either candidate, you will see a decline in your Federal Income Tax Bill. With either candidate, you will see a rise in the federal debt and federal deficit, or frankly put, government services will be on a credit card that is held by the Bank of China and other buyers of U.S. debt at reasonably low interest rates. The current administration calls itself "conservative" which apparently does not mean "fiscally conservative", and yet this administration never balanced the budget. The last person to balance the budget and impose "fiscally conservative" principals was Bill Clinton in 1996. Before that, the last "fiscally conservative" President was Richard Nixon in 1972.

The National Debt and Federal Deficit are issues that were ignored in the last two elections and are continually ignored. Who wants to hear the reason that we must raise taxes is that we were reckless and irresponsible? These issues won't win too many addressing this issue would not garner votes. The Deficit is basically the amount each year the government falls short of funds to operate. The National debt is the accumulation of public and private sector debt. Since there is no public outcry to correct this issue, we continue to spend more for government services than we take in from taxation.

American's with income between 161,000 and $250,000

The republican plan will give you tax relief in the amount of $4,380. Obama will give you tax relief of $2,789. For Americans in this category, the choice is leaning to the republicans. Over $1,000 more will be in your pocket if you vote for John. You may disagree with the war in Iraq, you may not like the growing federal deficit by the "non-fiscally conservative" the republicans, but you will have more money to spend on cars, house payments, even perhaps a second home. Receiving back $4,380! You could pay off all your credit card debt in two years with the amount of tax savings you will receive from the republicans plan. If you don't plan to vote Republican in this year's election; at least think about it. Taxes affect every day choices and lifestyle issues. What could be more important?

"IF YOU ARE EARNING MORE THAN $250,000 A YEAR, YOU SHOULD VOTE FOR THE REPUBLICAS!"

The Top 1%

The top 1% or the third standard deviation of any group is exceptional. This group accounts for the largest pool of income, talent and taxes in America. The group is quite large, about 3 million people. (Given a population base of 300 million) This group really runs the show (or the United States) with more economic power than the bottom 20% combined. How will the election affect you? It depends where in the top 1% you exist. Remember if we take the top 1% and isolate this group and take the top 1% of this group, or about 30,000, the tax impact is dramatic. If you are in the bottom 20% of this group, or about 600,000 people, the tax impact is not as dramatic. The top 1% of taxpayers in the U.S. pay a large share of Federal Income Taxes. This group is represented by Professionals such as Doctors and Lawyers, Business Owners, Mid-level and high-level executives etc.

High Income Americans with income between $250,000 and $603,000

The republicans plan will LOWER your tax bill by $7,871 a year. Obama will INCREASE your tax bill by $12. Clearly you should vote for the republicans-or should you? Is the $7,871 tax savings really material to your income statement? As your income grows greater than $227,000, the tax savings will represent less than 2% of your overall income. Perhaps other issues should be addressed as the extra cost of taxation is immaterial to your income. These issues are beyond the scope of this book and should be reviewed independently.

Higher Income with income between $603,000 and $2.9 million

Many people in this category include specialty physicians, attorneys who are experts in their fields, business owners and senior executives. Under BOTH plans, your tax bill will increase. Under The republicans, your tax bill will increase over $45,361. Under the Obama plan, your tax bill will increase $115,974. So whoever gets elected, be prepared to pay more in Federal income taxes; or meet with your tax advisor to set up retirement plans that will at least defer the current taxation that is about to hit your income statement. Look for Country club dues to level off, vacation home areas such as Aspen, Vail, Sun Valley to decline as well as the Florida real estate market. In addition, the specialty stores such as ones found on Worth Avenue in Palm Beach and Rodeo Drive in Beverly Hills may experience slightly reduced revenue.

Highest Income Americans with income of more than $2,900,000 per year

Many people in this category include CEOs, hedge fund managers, actors, money managers, entertainment personalities, sports figures, etc. Under either plan, your tax bill will increase. If you vote for the republicans, your taxes will go up $269,364 per year. If you vote for Obama, your tax bill will increase $701,885 per year. Much of the income that comes from this group, however, is not ordinary income, but rather capital gains and dividend income which are currently taxed at 15%. The income tax is sheltered through the use of Municipal Bonds and deferred through tax deferred annuities. Many have enjoyed tax free status of investments though private placement life insurance policies. The tax may increase on paper, but not in reality.

More significantly, these people benefit from the effect of working with larger sums of money. If you remember our conversations with typical taxpayers, in ten years $50,000 doubled to $100,000; $1,000,000 doubled to $200,000; $100,000,000 doubled to $200,000,000. See the "wealth effect"? Those at the top need lower tax rates? The low tax rates are what make the gap between the top 1% and the bottom 40% increase each year. It wasn't always this way. For most of our history the top marginal rate exceeded 70% per year. Wages were far more equitable and an executive position with a Fortune 500 corporation was not the equivalent of winning a sizable lottery. What was so bad? The economy grew. The nation prospered. People felt good about themselves, and their futures, college was very affordable. Marjorie knows about affordability. She put herself through the graduate tax program at USC herself. Total loans? She borrowed $1,500. That is affordable.

BOTTOM LINE: "IF YOU ARE MAKING MORE THAN $250,000 A YEAR, YOU SHOULD VOTE FOR THE REPUBLICANS!"

"What most people don't seem to realize is
that there is just as much money to be made
 out of the wreckage of a civilization as from the
building of one."

Margaret Mitchell, *Gone with the Wind,* 1936

TAXES ARE OBJECTIVE MATH PROBLEMS

No matter how we "brand" people, tax, fiscal, and economic policies affect every American. Income tax laws address three questions: "What is income? When is it income?", and "Who owns the income?" Excise taxes are fees charged to regulate and control everything from gasoline to tires. Then we also have the Estate and Gift Taxes. The purpose of taxes is to provide the funds we need to fulfill our obligations under the Constitution and under those programs put in place by Congress related to the government's responsibilities under the Constitution. The government actually has mandates to take care of the items listed in Article 2, Section 8 of the Constitution. It would be helpful for you to familiarize yourself with the specific tasks outlined. In addition, Congress has undertaken certain tasks that were not even thought of when the Constitution was drafted. The beauty of this document is that we can make these changes to accommodate new technology and new global considerations.

The point is that your vision for America should be the basis of choosing the nature of our tax system and the level of taxes we pay. Taxes are the price we pay for the privilege of being Americans. Taxes are our acknowledgment that we have the duty to support this country by supporting the laws we pass. Knee-jerk movements to cut taxes without considering what those taxes should be used for do not make any sense. We are in the fix we are in because for the past 28 years, Republicans have fostered this "cut taxes at all cost" mania that has essentially bankrupted the nation. Reagan started. He pushed tax cuts through and then did nothing to contain spending because the programs he wanted to cut were programs our citizens wanted to keep. What were we thinking? What was he thinking? What was Congress thinking? I have no idea. Apparently, we took a break from thinking and from accepting responsibility for meeting our obligations as a nation.

Tax policy and economics are pure math problems. If you earn **A**, subtract expenses **B** you end up with **C**. Tax of x% is paid on **C**, and you have **D** left over.

What are you going to do with **D**? Save it, spend it, or give it away. Those are really the choices. Economists build assumptions into what you are going to do with **D**. If you save it, then there is capital formation. If you spend it, there is consumption.

If tax rates rise, you will have less of **D**. If tax rates fall, you will have more of **D**. If the government borrows money to pay the tax you should have paid, International markets will react, your cost of goods will go up and you will have less of **D**.

Why will this happen? Let's play a game. I own country a called U.S.A. You own country "C" called Canada. Our currency is on par where $1 US = $1 C. I decide to "print money" so my citizens can purchase your goods at a discount. I double my money supply. My citizens are happy as they now go into your country and buy goods cheaper as I print more and more money just for them. How do you think country "C' is going to react? Will they say great, come buy us up cheap? Or will they raise their prices to reflect our "printing money"?

It doesn't take Albert Einstein to figure this one out. When we "printed money" to stimulate the economy without producing more goods or services, we invited the international community to sell to us at cheaper rates. Now they may do this for awhile, until they figure this one out. When they do, watch our dollar drop and price of goods increase. There is a "lag" time between the time a country prints money and other countries figure out the gaming of the currency; hence we may experience a short term "economic high", only to be followed by a reality check. Printing money can have a "Meth" effect on our economy. Deficits have a "meth" effect on our economy. Increasing the National Debt is the result of this effect which can be hidden-but for how long? Does this demonstrate sound economic policies in your mind? Then, to compound the problem, we use the money we borrow to buy oil from countries harboring the terrorists who are the object of the war on terror. The Saudis may be friends with the Bush family, but they have repeatedly demonstrated that they are not friends of the average American.

We pay many different kinds of taxes. While generally, politicians focus on the Income Tax, the truth is that "Payroll Taxes", the taxes every wage earner pays to support Social Security, start at the first dollar you earn. The combined rate between employer and employee is 15.3 percent. Earned income is taxed at that rate up to the cap, which is $102,000 this year. The cap is adjusted for inflation. The reason this tax is structured this way, is that Republicans generally oppose "transfer" payments. Transfer payments are Robin Hood payments. Someone may pay more into the fund than they will ever receive. The Republicans consider transfer payment to be "socialistic" payments. Heaven forbid that we should expect those who are relatively well off to contribute to meeting the needs of less affluent citizens.

There is only one problem with that thinking. Since 1980, the Republican administrations have adopted tax policies that tend to work just in reverse. The wealth gap has become the Grand Canyon and the top one percent of taxpayers have seen their incomes increase to $867,800 in 2004, from $314,000 in 1979, according to the Congressional Budget Office. Why do people keep choosing 1979 as the base for comparison? In 1980, Ronald Reagan was elected and the tax rates were lowered dramatically for the upper income brackets. At the same time the government began running enormous deficits, because we actually have responsibilities we must meet. Since that time the top one percent has seen their incomes rise $533,800 or 176% while the lowest quintile experienced an increase of $800, or 6%. For many reasons, the tax cuts for the rich have benefitted the rich and left the rest of us in rather precarious circumstances.

In view of the tremendous transfer of wealth from the bottom 99% to the upper 1%, transferring the money back to the people would seem appropriate. The top 1% in wealth in this country control 38% of all the assets in the nation, while the bottom 40% control only 0.2% (that is two-tenths of one percent) of all the assets in the U.S.

Change in Real After-Tax Income 1979-2004

Income Category	1979	2004	Percent Change 1979-2004	Dollar Change 1979-2004
Lowest 5th	$13,900	$14,700	6%	$800
2nd fifth	28,000	32,700	17%	4,700
Middle 5th	39,900	48,400	21%	8,500
4th fifth	52,300	67,600	29%	15,300
Top fifth	92,100	155,200	69%	63,100
Top 1%	314,000	867,800	176%	553,800

"We want a society where people are free to make choices, to make mistakes, to be generous and compassionate. This is what we mean by a moral society; not a society where the state is responsible for everything; and no one is responsible for the state."

Margaret Thatcher, speech, 1977

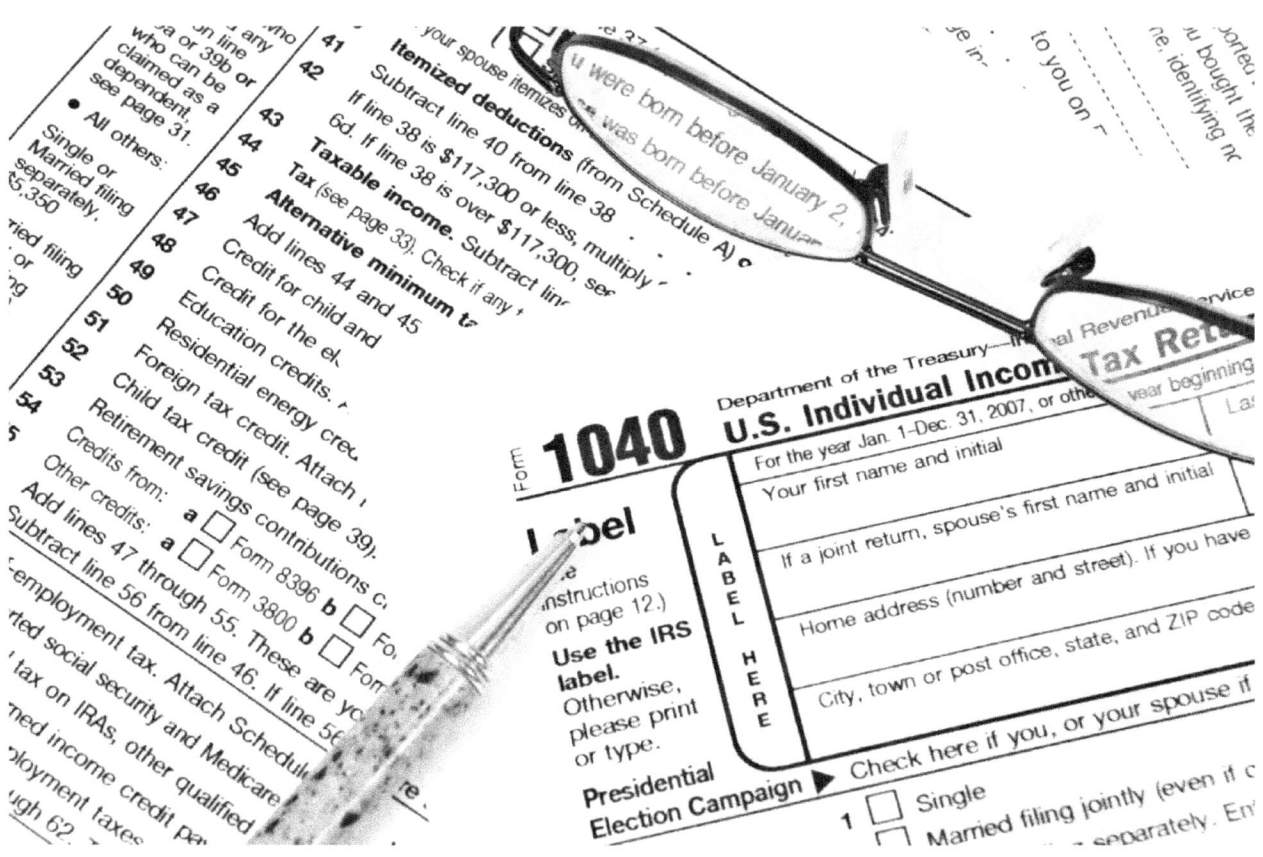

THE FEDERAL INCOME TAX

In order to better understand the context of the current circumstances, it would be useful to review the history of the income tax and historic tax rates. There has always been interplay between the income tax and the Social Security and Medicare taxes, often referred to as payroll taxes. These taxes are withheld from each paycheck received by employees. Hence the name. Chart 2 shows the top and bottom income tax rates from 1913 when the tax was ratified until 2000.

Historical Income Tax Rates & Brackets

| Calendar Year | Tax Rates 1 | | | |
| | Bottom bracket | | Top bracket | |
	Rate (percent)	Taxable Income Up to	Rate (percent)	Taxable Income over
1913-15	1	20,000	7	500,000
1916	2	20,000	15	2,000,000
1917	2	2,000	67	2,000,000
1918	6	4,000	77	1,000,000
1919-20	4	4,000	73	1,000,000
1921	4	4,000	73	1,000,000
1922	4	4,000	56	200,000
1923	3	4,000	56	200,000
1924	[2] 1.5	4,000	46	500,000
1925-28	[2] 1?	4,000	25	100,000
1929	[2] 4?	4,000	24	100,000
1930-31	[2] 1?	4,000	25	100,000
1932-33	4	4,000	63	1,000,000
1934-35	[3] 4	4,000	63	1,000,000
1936-39	[3] 4	4,000	79	5,000,000
1940	[3] 4.4	4,000	81.1	5,000,000
1941	[3] 10	2,000	81	5,000,000
1942-43[4]	[3] 19	2,000	88	200,000
1944-45	23	2,000	[5] 94	200,000
1946-47	19	2,000	[5] 86.45	200,000
1948-49	16.6	4,000	[5] 82.13	400,000
1950	17.4	4,000	[5] 91	400,000

1951	20.4	4,000	[5] 91	400,000
1952-53	22.2	4,000	[5] 92	400,000
1954-63	20	4,000	[5] 91	400,000
1964	16	1,000	77	400,000
1965-67	14	1,000	70	200,000
1968	14	1,000	[6] 75.25	200,000
1969	14	1,000	[6] 77	200,000
1970	14	1,000	[6] 71.75	200,000
1971	14	1,000	[7] 70	200,000
1972-78	[8] 14	1,000	[7] 70	200,000
1979-80	814	2,100	[7] 70	212,000
1981	[8] [9] 13.825	2,100	[7] [9] 69.125	212,000
1982	[8] 12	2,100	50	106,000
1983	[8] 11	2,100	50	106,000
1984	[8] 11	2,100	50	159,000
1985	[8] 11	2,180	50	165,480
1986	[8] 11	2,270	50	171,580
1987	[8] 11	3,000	38.5	90,000
1988	[8] 15	29,750	[10] 28	29,750
1989	[8] 15	30,950	[10] 28	30,950
1990	[8] 15	32,450	[10] 28	32,450
1991	[8] 15	34,000	31	82,150
1992	[8] 15	35,800	31	86,500
1993	[8] 15	36,900	39.6	250,000
1994	[8] 15	38,000	39.6	250,000
1995	[8] 15	39,000	39.6	256,500
1996	[8] 15	40,100	39.6	263,750
1997	[8] 15	41,200	39.6	271,050
1998	[8] 15	42,350	39.6	278,450
1999	[8] 15	43,050	39.6	283,150
2000	[8] 15	43,850	39.6	288,350

1 Taxable income excludes zero bracket amount from 1977 through 1986. Rates shown apply only to married persons filing joint returns beginning in 1948. Does not include either the add on minimum tax on preference items (1970-1982) or the alternative minimum tax (1979-present). Also, does not include the effects of the various tax benefit phase-outs (e.g. the personal exemption phase-out). From 1922 through 1986 and from 1991 forward, lower rates applied to long-term capital gains.

2 After earned-income deduction equal to 25 percent of earned income.

3 After earned-income deduction equal to 10 percent of earned income.

4 Exclusive of Victory Tax.

5 Subject to the following maximum effective rate limitations.

[year and maximum rate (in percent)] 1944-45 –90; 1946-47 –85.5; 1948-49 –77.0; 1950 –87.0; 1951 –87.2; 1952-53 –88.0; 1954-63 –87.0.

6 Includes surcharge of 7.5 percent in 1968, 10 percent in 1969, and 2.6 percent in 1970.

7 Earned income was subject to maximum marginal rates of 60 percent in 1971 and 50 percent from 1972 through 1981.

8 Beginning in 1975, a refundable earned-income credit is allowed for low-income individuals.

9 After tax credit is 1.25 percent against regular tax.

10 The benefit of the first rate bracket is eliminated by an increased rate above certain thresholds. The phase-out range of the benefit of the first rate bracket was as follows: Taxable income between $71,900 and $149,250 in 1988; taxable income between $74,850 and $155,320 in 1989; and taxable income between $78,400 and $162,770 in 1990. The phase-out of the benefit the first rate bracket was repealed for taxable years beginning after December 31, 1990. This added 5 percentage points to the marginal rate for those by the phase-out, producing a 33 percent effective rate.

Source: Joint Committee on Taxation, Overview of Present Law and Economic Analysis Relating to Marginal Tax Rates and the President's Individual Income Tax Rate Proposals (JCX-6-01), March 6, 2001.

Now there are some interesting facts reported in this chart. First of all, you will notice that each time we were engaged in a war, the tax rates increased dramatically. This is the **ONLY** administration to both instigate a war, *and* put it on the credit card. Somehow, this country became the most prosperous, well-run, and most creative and best educated country in the world with the highest marginal tax rates between 70% and 90% for most of the time until 1980. Since 1980, we have lost millions of jobs overseas, the tax burden on the middle class has increased under every Republican administration, the middle class is struggling to make ends meet, and health care costs are out of control. Bill Clinton had balanced the budget, created eight years of solid growth and prosperity, and attempted to implement Social Security reform and health care reform, apparently, according to Republican thinking, in spite of somewhat higher tax rates. His reform efforts were held hostage by the unyielding obsession with his regrettable behavior, and the nation's ten-year olds learned more than they really wanted to know about sexual matters. Executive compensation is completely out of control and hedge fund traders are taxed at 15% from their trading income which has been in the $200 MILLION to $300 MILLION range. This is fair? Bill Clinton was the first President to balance the budget, and have a growth economy since Richard Nixon.

Tax History

When the income tax amendment was ratified in 1913, as a country, we were in a very different place. Most taxpayers were family farmers, and factory workers. Labor unions were beginning to attempt to assert workers' rights and the industrial age was off to a good start. There was a general consensus that the wealthy, for all their robber-baron behavior, had a responsibility to meet their share of providing the foundation for good government and a healthy economy. The highest marginal rate began at seven percent on taxable income over $500,000. During World War I, the highest rate increased to between 67% and 77%. Then during the Roaring Twenties the highest marginal rate dropped back to 25%. This was followed by modest increases until the rate increased to 63% of income over $1 million. These higher marginal rates continued during the lead up to World War II. These higher marginal rates continued until 1982, as you can see on the chart. Remember Ronald Reagan was elected in 1980, promising to lower tax rates for everyone. The tax rates dropped to 50% on the highest income bracket and then eventually to 28% in 1988. Bush I failed to be reelected because he reneged on his promise of "No new taxes." He raised the highest rate to 31% from 28%.

Under Bill Clinton, the highest rate was raised to 39.6% on income over $250,000 slowly increasing to $288,350 by 2000. Over that period of time, the other thing that happened was that executive compensation increased dramatically and American jobs began to migrate out of the country. Then when we elected Bush II the highest marginal rate dropped again, and the flow of jobs overseas accelerated. Why am I telling you this?

Here is one consideration. When the highest marginal tax rate was between 70 and 91%, there was very little incentive to increase income beyond the levels of $200,000 to $400,000. With tax rates that high, most of the additional income was going to pay taxes. Americans have never been fond of taxes. They just used to accept taxes as part of being an American and there was enormous pride in the high standards, efficient transportation, communication, and educational institutions in this country. Our freeways were the best in the world. They were solid, well engineered most of the time, and safe. We responded to the Russians going into outer space by beating them to the Moon, in spite of their sizable head start. In 1970, the chief executive officer on average earned 50 times more than the lowest paid factory worker. There was balance and a sense of fairness to tax and fiscal policy. There was a genuine sense that the CEO could not succeed without the support of the rank and file. They were a team. Workers spent their entire careers at one company, and company loyalty was essential to success.

Slowly, over the next twenty years that sense of loyalty, mutual respect and shared destiny eroded to the "winner take all" economy. From what I have observed, the lower marginal rates were an essential factor in this evolution. The Center on Budget and Policy Priorities issued a report on January 23, 2007, New CBO Data Show Income Inequality Continues to Widen". "The CBO data also indicate that the growth in income disparities since 1979 largely reflects changes in before-tax income." (Page 4) They go on to observe that the disparity increased when the rate was lowered but declined during the years when the marginal rate increased and cuts and credits for the lowest brackets increased. I will give you an illustration. Our family spent a summer in Greenwich, during the summer of 1990. I will never forget reading the story of a factory closed in the northeast. The woman vice-president earned a salary of $7,000,000 annually. The annual cost of running the factory was $6,000,000. She closed the factory down and sent the jobs to a cheaper foreign location. At that time, executives were making about 500 times the salaries of the rank and file workers. The highest marginal tax rate was 28% on income over $32,450. Why not take the income?

We see a similar situation in the medical field. You will have a group of doctors making $300,000 to $500,000 or more. They fire their medical staff. Outsource clerical support at a much lower cost. The benefit? They can establish generous pension plans for themselves and they have no employees to include. If the marginal rates on high incomes were higher, there would be less incentive to take these actions.

Today we have our modern version of the tax and spend society. Taxes are collected through an inefficient and complicated process. The tax law consists of the boring Internal Revenue Code, Regulations, Revenue Rulings, Revenue Procedures, Private Letter Rulings, Tax Court decisions, tax forms, tax instructions, tax books and tax police a/k/a the tax auditor who attempts to keep the taxpayer from cheating or abusing the system. The auditor can be challenged, and the issue goes to appeals. If the appeal is challenged, the issue goes to tax court. If you have a tax attorney and the financial means to pay the tax and file for a refund, you can go to a Federal District Court instead of the Tax Court. In Federal District Court, you may even have a jury! You do not get a jury before the Tax Court.

You may also appeal decisions from either court to one of the eleven Circuit Courts of Appeal; and then finally to the Supreme Court of the United States.

Now for all those "Tax Protestors" who say the tax laws are unconstitutional, do yourself a favor-GIVE IT UP. First, these laws are in the Constitution, we even have a constitutional amendment allowing for taxes. Second, the Constitution is subject to interpretation and is guided by our Supreme Court who does not buy these idiotic arguments that the taxes are unconstitutional as they are not "voluntary". And if you are so "Proud to be an American", why are you not eager to pay your share of the cost of running your country? Third, seek professional help. No not tax help, mental help. An unfair system, perhaps, an unconstitutional system-NO!

Tax policy has reflected the values and vision of Americans through the years since 1913 when it was first assessed. As you can see from the table, up until 1980, the tax rates on the wealthy were basically confiscatory. This means that over the threshold amount usually around $400,000, there was not too much incentive to increase one's income, unless you wanted to pay it over to the government in taxes. Many of you were not around when executive compensation was only 50 times rank and file compensation. You do not remember when the distribution of wealth was broader and in general average people could go to college, live in decent homes, drive decent cars and look forward to a nice retirement. That was the promise I grew up with, and in the past 28 years, that promise has been taken from me, and those in my age group through our own folly, ignorance, and irresponsibility.

The Sixteenth Amendment, establishing the Income Tax, went into effect February 3, 1913. We had discovered that duties on imports did not raise enough revenue to meet the nation's needs. This was felt to be a fair way of collecting taxes because it was based on the ability to pay. What a novel and noble idea.

For the next 67 years that principle pretty much determined the tax rates applied to collect enough revenue to meet the obligations created by the Budget. When we were at war, the rates went up. When we were at peace, they usually went down. In general, for incomes over about $400,000 were taxed at rates between 70% and 90%. The country, in general, prospered. There was money for real roads, good schools, research to put a man on the moon, and somehow we survived without health insurance. Rich people paid more and poor people paid what they could. Doctors were there to take care of their patients, not make buckets of money. They were generally pretty happy with better than average income, and no insurance companies to deal with. At least that is what I remembered about growing up. Richard Nixon even balanced the budget, while withdrawing from Viet Nam. What happened?

Well, there was the first Energy Crisis, which led to rationing in the form of buying gas on odd or even days, determined by whether the last number on your license plate was "even" or "odd". Still, gas prices were relatively low. Unfortunately, Jimmy Carter, who tried to guide us down the correct path failed to persuade the D.C. establishment to join him and we ended up with Ronald Reagan. His administration was the beginning of the deterioration in the promise of America for everyone. He gave us the "Trickle-Down" theory. The nation has not been the same since.

We present here some of the thinking that got us to where we find ourselves.

Goofy Theory #1: Trickle-Down Theory

Tax breaks for the wealthy will "trickle down" to the lower and middle classes. Who would buy this? Let's conduct an "unscientific" experiment with a 5 year old and a 2 year old. Give the 5 year old 10 M&M candies and tell him whatever he does not want to eat let it "trickle down" to his younger brother. How many M&Ms did little brother eat? Now let's try dividing the M&Ms: 5 for the older brother, and 5 for the younger brother. How many M&Ms did the brothers eat? Well, the bigger brother may beat up the little brother and eaten them all-but at least the little brother had a chance. You can intervene and stop the conflict or not. Who would sell this idea to the American Public? Well Ronald Reagan was a great communicator and we . . .

"Thinking to get at once all the gold the goose could give, he killed it and opened it only to find—nothing.—Aesop, "The Goose with the Golden Eggs", *Fables*

Goofy Theory #2: If You Raise Capital Gains Taxes, You Will Collect Less Tax Revenue, AND Discourage Investment.

Right. This statement is made by mathematically challenged pundits who, if they studied vectors, matrices and limits, could prove to themselves that the statement is mathematically false. The argument goes that if you increase taxes you will collect less revenue because the higher tax deters capital investment and inhibits capital growth and formation. Empirical evidence is gathered to find the one time when lower taxes generated more activity and resulted in more tax revenue.

Let's run a basic model. We establish capital gains rates at 50%. Each transaction generates $10,000 in revenue. We deterred transactions because the rate was so high, we only had 2 transactions and collected $20,000. Next we lower the tax rate to 25%. The average tax collection is now $5,000 per transaction as the rate is lowered. Due to the lower rate there were 5 transactions and we collected $25,000. The overall collection went up!

Using this model, we decided to lower rates again to 0%. The average collection now is 0%. Now, we doubled our transactions to 10 transactions and collected $0.

Hummm…….lowering the tax rate did not increase revenue. There is an optimal rate between 100% and zero, but in all cases you cannot just keep decreasing taxes and come to the optimal rate. In any case, you must work a model with various assumptions similar to price volume profit analysis when pricing products. You will eventually find an "optimal tax" level. The increase in capital gains collection is "assumed " to be due to more capital gains transactions due to the lower rate, however it could also be accounted for by tax attorneys and tax accountants moving transactions from higher income tax rates to capital gains. In many cases, an optimal tax rate for one type of transaction does not translate into higher total tax revenue. In order to have a FAIR tax, the marginal rates for corporate tax, individual tax and capital gains tax should be the same rate. If they are not the same, the government is opening up the ability to "game" the system by tax attorneys and tax accountants. These activities are difficult to police, keep tax attorneys and accountants employed, and increase the complexity of the tax laws because Congress is constantly changing the law to close the "loophole". The increased cost to the economy as a whole is not worth the differential in rates. The other problem is that the majority of people out there would rather pay an attorney than pay the tax.

Goofy Theory #3: If You Have an Estate Tax, The Heirs of Small Business Owners and Farmers Will Lose the Business/Farm.

This is perhaps the goofiest theory ever sold to the American public. In fact, a recent study showed 72% of Americans thought the "death tax" was unfair. Great sales job, wealthy Republicans. Let's look at the facts.

The Marital Deduction covers all the tax when a spouse dies, so there are NO TAXES (except if you live in a state which has a "state estate tax" or an "inheritance tax" and does not have a deduction-consult with your tax advisor). When the surviving spouse dies, in 2009 $7 million will pass to the next generation without any tax. In order to have the entire $7 million, you have to have made the appropriate arrangements way in advance. Consult with a qualified attorney.

How big is your business? Is it worth $7 million or more?

How big is your farm? Is it worth $7 million or more?

If the answer is yes, you need to consult a tax advisor. If the answer is no, you still need to consult a tax advisor to make sure you receive the entire credit which will allow you to pass $7 million with no taxes (once again, state taxes may be imposed by some states).

Now let us look at the problem again. Seventy-two percent of the electorate **think** that the estate tax is unfair. There are so many myths out there that our voters believe. People should be able to inherit $7 million tax free, for literally doing nothing except treating mom and dad, or Uncle Harry well. At the same time, the caregiver who works hard all year long and makes $9.00 an hour ($18,000 a year) and will pay 15.3% in Social Security and Medicare taxes on every dime she makes. She is working, and making a contribution to society, taking care of Uncle Harry who has all his money in municipal bonds, so he pays no federal income taxes.

Now at this time we need to look at abortion and gay rights so we can bypass the inequality of the tax system and look at values…etc….etc..

Please -- one discussion at a time. We are not going to end that argument in our collective lifetimes anyway. Why waste your time?

During the Sixties and Seventies, Congress actually realized that the family farm was a problem, so they changed the law. No one has lost a family farm due to the Estate Tax in decades. As we discuss later, this is a purely voluntary tax, unless you fail to plan properly and make the proper arrangements. If you have several million dollars, then you can well afford to consult with an attorney and prevent your heirs from being disinherited because of federal taxes. Besides, when they collect any tax, you will be dead.

Now, the Federal Income Tax is once again under attack. So the question becomes, "How do you propose to meet the obligations we have chosen as a country?"

This is the system we have. It seems logical that those who have more should pay more because they can, and because their success has been possible thanks to our education system, our financial institutions, our robust economy and our legal system. The principle used to be that with more success comes more responsibility.

Taxes are not necessarily the problem. The financial plight of the Middle Class has many contributors. The repeated failure of various administrations to negotiate for better trading terms, the fiscal policies of the Fed, the focus on the housing industry to keep the economy expanding led to an unbalanced economy. Greater prosperity did not translate into more collection of revenue. Tax cuts for the wealthy were paid for by the rest of us. Wake up America.

"You take my life,

when you take the means whereby I live."

William Shakespeare, *The Merchant of Venice*, 1596

PAYROLL TAXES

Payroll taxes are paid by every working American from dollar one. These are the taxes withheld to contribute to Social Security and Medicare. Employees pay 7.65% tax on their wages. The employer also pays 7.65% on employee wages to the IRS. This tax is paid within two days of the date employees are paid under a federal collection to a designated bank as the depository. There is a 25% penalty on late payments. Politicians usually like to ignore this tax. In many respects the tax is regressive, it treats all taxpayers the same regardless of their income. Further, while the tax has no "floor", or amount up to which the tax is not levied, there is a cap at $102,000 for 2008. This means that those making over $102,000 only pay the tax on their income up to $102,000. They continue to pay the Medicare Tax on all income however. These funds are allocated to the Social Security Trust Fund for payment to retirees, the disabled who qualify, and surviving spouses and children.

This tax is a pain. It was actuarially unsound when imposed; and it is destined for destruction if remedial action is not taken. Social Security was created as one segment of a three part program for funding working people's retirement. The first leg was the defined benefit pension plan provided by the employer. Those are going by the wayside daily. A defined benefit pension is extremely expensive to fund. The second leg was personal savings. Yes, dears, there was a time when even working people had something left over to save. Profit sharing plans, and 401(k) plans provide a way to save without paying income tax on the money contributed to the plan, and the money is safe for retirement, even if one must file bankruptcy. Unfortunately, given the relatively depressed compensation levels for the average worker, and the increasing cost of living, very few employees have anything left to contribute. Many companies have already frozen or terminated their defined benefit plans and replaced them with 401(k) plans. The problem is that most people have no idea how much they will need for a comfortable retirement, and most people have very little to contribute anyway. What does this mean? Many of us will be working into our seventies if we are healthy just to have enough to survive. Even with that most Americans will retire in poverty. Finally, the Social Security program is a looming tsunami that must be addressed responsibly YESTERDAY. Congress and various presidents have passed this issue around like a "hot potato" because the solution will require sacrifice from each of us.

This tax is the highest it has ever been, and burdens employers and employees. The rigid payment dates give start-up companies or companies experiencing a down turn no room to maneuver or buy time. If the company has no access to credit at the time of a cash shortage, they cannot pay their workers. They have to shut their doors. Many employers are put in the position of either paying the tax late, or shutting down.

When data is analyzed about who pays more in taxes, the payroll tax on working Americans is usually left out of the analysis to skew the results. Even at the 15% marginal rate, employees and employers pay an additional 15% on each dollar of earned income up to $102,000. Even if you do not have enough income to pay federal income tax, you must still pay a 15% Social Security and Medicare Tax.

Why is this? When Franklin Delano Roosevelt set this system up, it was a "pay as you go" system. The workers today pay the benefits of the people who have retired. The assumption was that the economy always expands and so this will work out. When you go to retire, you hope that enough people are working and contributing enough to pay for your benefits. Oh my glory! What kind of a stupid system is that? The crisis is that the Baby Boomers far exceed the number of people who will be working when Boomers retire. Moreover, the costs of health care have become staggering because we are not producing enough doctors, so they can and do charge outrageous fees for their services.

There is one other interesting aspect to payroll taxes. There is no floor, no amount below which the tax is not assessed. There has always been a "cap". Above the cap, no tax is assessed. Right now that cap is $102,000. This amount is adjusted for inflation. Eliminating the cap would probably make the system solvent without any other action. Another loophole that must be closed is the "K-1" payments made by Subchapter S corporations to the business owner/employee. As it stands, these payments to business owners who work in their own company are not subject to Social Security tax. The owner must pay income tax, but not the payroll taxes. This loophole makes no sense. Earned income is income earned in the process of providing products or services to a third party. Salaries and wages are also earned income. If you own a Subchapter S corporation they can reduce their salaries so that they pay little Social Security tax and then pay themselves a distribution reported on a K-1. The K-1 income is not subject to Social Security taxes. Is this fair? Does this make any sense? I don't think so.

Warren Buffet observed that his secretary paid a higher percentage of her income in taxes than he did. The reason? Investment income, dividends and interest, is taxed at a 15% rate. There are no payroll taxes. The secretary must pay the 15.3% plus her income tax. If she is in the 15% bracket, her overall tax rate is 30%. Warren Buffet's marginal rate is 15%. This is fair?

Not only that, but the secretary is working so that Warren Buffet is paid his Social Security benefit and is covered by Medicare. What a country! Working people must support retired billionaires.

"Coming together is a beginning; keeping together is progress; working together is success."

Henry Ford

THE CORPORATE INCOME TAX

The corporate income tax is another area where the two candidates disagree. Obama would like to keep the tax where it is, which is the same level as the federal personal income tax. The republicans wants to lower the corporate tax by 10% making a disparity between personal income taxes and corporate taxes.

Which plan is better? It depends on who you ask. The corporate tax was put in place to be equivalent to the Federal income tax to stop the gaming of the tax system by tax attorneys (like myself) and CPAs. A good simple example is as follows. Let's say you have a person with $100,000 income. You will pay tax of $35,000 as an individual or tax of $35,000 as a corporation. Given these facts, there is no reason to create a company. (Under the current rules there are some incentives such as payroll taxes and different lower marginal rates for non-personal service companies).

Let's say we adopt the republican plan. We now create a corporation and pay our client a salary of $20,000 which he or she will pay income tax at 35% or $7,000. We have the corporation pay the tax on the remaining $80,000 or $20,000 for a total tax liability of $27,000 as opposed to $35,000 - and we save our client $8,000 in taxes.

Brilliant-YES! These policies are the full employment program for tax attorneys and CPAs. Thanks The republicans. Now how does this help stimulate innovation? Well, my client ends up with more money to spend. This plan also allows me to set up simple corporations to allow small business owners to shelter more of their hard earned income. Large corporations will just pay less in corporate income taxes, which could translate into higher dividends for their wealthy shareholders.

Or… the savings could be squandered on more and bigger cars, second homes, etc. Now how does it help you, the employee who makes less than $100,000? It doesn't!

Now we own small businesses. One business is a personal service business. For the first time, in 2008 we are enjoying some prosperity. From our standpoint, the corporate income tax for small businesses is purely voluntary and here is why. Retirement is mainly left to private industry. In a small business, the owners can make significant contributions to their qualified retirement plans, provide health benefits, and other employee benefits, pay bonuses and pretty much eliminate taxable income at the corporate level. There seems to be one huge obstacle to providing generous retirement benefits to their employees. The business owners by and large, don't want to give anything to their employees. At the 35% tax rate, if the contribution to the employees exceeds 15-20% of the total contribution (meaning that 80-85% of the contribution benefits the owner) they won't establish that plan. They will choose the least expensive option, unless they actually want to provide for the employees. If you lower the corporate income tax rate, they will not even look at qualified plans. Further, corporations have so many loopholes that they often do not pay taxes at the 35% rate. Providing health insurance and retirement benefits for employees is not what makes life difficult for small businesses and their employees. The payroll taxes and the collection system imposed by the government are the tough hurdles. Further, each state imposes a variety of taxes on businesses. Usually, these taxes are not very large, but again, they can pose a problem for cash strapped start-ups. What would benefit small business owners is access to cash. If you don't have perfect credit, you can get personal credit cards at 20% interest, but you can't get a loan for or even a credit card for the company. If you don't have a profit, you pay no tax. Even if you break even during those first five years, you will not be able to get credit at an affordable interest rate.

Obama has several proposals to increase access to capital for small and micro-businesses, especially in rural areas. These communities need some program to help them provide incomes for their residents and a future for their young people. Northwestern Washington State is a perfect example. The entire state has benefitted by the relatively low cost of electricity. What we need are more clean, high tech jobs. There are already companies producing biofuels. The entire eastern half of the state is a perfect corridor for wind energy. Those new jobs would boost the entire region. Drilling for oil helps Alaska.

The "trickle down theory" was a theory of economics and taxation proposed by Arthur Laffer and Robert Mundell among others, during the 1970s. Mundell later disavowed it, however Laffer has made a fortune from promoting this mythical system. First of all, the economists made this theory up. I think it could work in an emerging economy. However, ours is a mature, very complex economy. The idea that cutting taxes for the wealthiest will create more spending seemed "voodoo economics" to Bush senior before he was elected as Reagan's Vice President. Turns out that he was very likely correct. For more information on Reagan, read about the Tax Reform Act of 1986 and the subsequent collapse of the real estate market and the savings and loan associations that followed. In addition to the increasing deficit and making contributions to pension plans less attractive, the "Reform Act" had the effect of making savings less attractive and overpaying top executives very attractive. Moreover, the "fiscally conservative" Reagan was no Richard Nixon; and never balanced the budget opting for more debt, and more debt, and more debt, etc.

In any event, with all political commentary aside, the decrease in corporate income tax only meant more gamesmanship for attorneys and CPAs. The trickle down theory promoted by Reagan (with all apologies to Louis XVI of France and his wife Marie Antoinette who really did like this theory) doesn't work. The theory will create greater economic disparity, which it already has, and make the economic segments even more difficult to traverse. However, we may like having different classes of Americans. Remember, the British like their royalty, why cannot we have our own royal class? We would have Super Wealthy, Wealthy, Merely Affluent as opposed to Kings, Dukes, and Barons. Actually, we already have such "Royalty". They are called "Celebrities".

Romney lowers the corporate income tax -- Obama leaves the rate at 35%. Bottom line:

"IF YOU ARE A CORPORATION, YOU SHOULD VOTE FOR THE REPUBLICANS!" (of course corporations can't vote)

"The ultimate measure of a man is not where he stands in moments of comfort and convenience, but where he stands at times of challenge and controversy."

Martin Luther King, Jr.

THE TAX ON CAPITAL GAINS

This tax is low relative to the income tax. The maximum rate is 15%. The tax rate was higher before George Bush took office. He lowered the tax to "stimulate the economy". What was the result? There are too many factors to reach a conclusion, but it is clear that his overall policies resulted in higher debt, fewer jobs, more disparity between rich and poor Americans, a lifeless stock market and a costly war.

Money Manager

Imagine you make all your money through savvy investments, which can be a full time job. You earn $100,000 in capital gains. Your tax bill is about $15,000 or 15%. You did not produce one product or provide any service for this country, but you did allocate capital in and out of stocks, bonds and real estate. You managed money and were rewarded for this and your tax bill always comes out at 15% or lower. No Social Security Tax, no need for a pension, you are making astronomical income.

The Small Owner

Imagine you work long hours, like the money manager. You also allocate capital, but also labor as you has employees and land as you either rent or own real estate. You have a successful year and you earn an additional $100,000, but unlike the money manager, you pay $35,000 in taxes because all the income is considered "earned income" and not treated as "capital gain". Not only that; you pay an additional 7.65% in Social Security and Medicare taxes not to mention state income taxes. In many states the capital gains are taxed the same as in the federal system.

The tax policy of the United States is that the earnings from capital is more sacred than the earnings from working without capital or "earned income" such as salaries, independent contracting work etc. If you produce products such as computers, airplanes, cars, and so on, your tax rate is higher than if you purchase property and resell it. Does this make any sense?

The farmer produces a crop for $200,000 in sales. His cost to produce the crop is $100,000. The farmer has a gain of $100,000 and the farmer pays taxes of $35,000.

Why does a money manager have a lower amount of tax than the farmer? Is his "crop" more valuable?

The Obama Plan

Accordingly, Mr. Obama has a plan to raise this tax to 25-28%, the tax during the Clinton era where the greatest boom occurred in the financial markets in the U.S. What does the Institute for Research on the Economics of Taxation say about the Obama plan? "Mr. Obama's tax hike would knock off $2.5 trillion in capital formation over five years or nearly 2% of gross domestic product". The problem with the Institute is they have no evidence to base this opinion on and reach a conclusion that is contrary to history. In many cases, there would be less incentive to sell stocks due to the higher tax rate, and this would actually create stability in the marketplace. The empirical evidence of this actually occurred during the eight year Clinton administration. There is no evidence that the lower capital gains tax had a positive effect on our economy. In fact, during the Bush administration, the stock market went nowhere over the eight-year period he was in office. Portfolios remained stagnant over eight years. There was a run up or increase in the housing market, only to face a dramatic fall that affects negatively the financial services industry.

BOTTOM LINE: IF YOU HAVE SUBSTANTIAL DIVIDEND AND CAPITAL GAIN INCOME, VOTE FOR THE REPUBLICANS!

"The mass of men worry themselves into nameless graves, while here and there a great unselfish soul forgets himself into immortality."

Ralph Waldo Emerson

THE FEDERAL ESTATE TAX

The Federal estate tax occurs once upon death and is based upon the net worth of the individual at death. If you are married, there is an unlimited marital deduction which means the spouse of the deceased person will not pay any tax. If you are a child who will inherit the estate, you may or may not pay any "death tax" depending on the size of the estate. Since 1981, when Reagan introduced the "unified credit" an increasing portion of the estate has been exempt from taxation so that the heirs receive a substantial inheritance free of tax. The tax was considered a means of recouping value compounding on the assets over a long period of time. The logic was that had the assets been sold during the lifetime of the testator (dead person) a certain amount of capital gains taxes would have been paid. This was considered fair to the heirs because in effect they were now free to dispose of the assets and realize the gain. The heirs also received a step-up in the taxable value of the assets as of the date of death or six months later, whichever was more advantageous to the heirs.

Then politicians came along and started calling it a "death tax" -- selling the American public on the evils of taxing millionaires. Why only poor people pay taxes Leona Helmsley would say, and the push to exempt millionaires from taxes continued. George W. Bush pushed through the product that was purchased by the American public: no taxes for the rich. (Remember only poor people should pay taxes, perhaps that is the reason they are poor.) Let's eliminate the "death tax" became the battle cry for "equity" in the federal tax system. In many cases, the assets in the estate had been inherited, and the credit covered the estate tax, hence no taxes were paid on these funds. In some cases, the increase in the value of the estate was never realized as the assets were capital gains that were never sold. Whatever the amount, the heirs did not work for these assets. They were members of the "luck sperm club" which is the reason the assets would end up in his or her hands. How large can the amount you receive tax free? How about $7 million dollars?

Here is the point. If you work every day and earn $7 million, you will pay about $2,100,000 in income taxes. If you are a member of the "lucky sperm club" and inherit $7,000,000, you will pay no income taxes, no estate taxes, and no Social Security or Medicare taxes.

Our policy is quite clear, it is better to inherit money than work for it. Work becomes a four letter word when this policy is adopted. Tax policy should reward work and effort. Tax policy should look at where you are going, not where you came from. Tax policy should reward the thrifty and industrious; not the lucky sperm societies that exist in Palm Beach.

The Obama Estate Tax Plan

"Everyone should be able to inherit $10 million without the burden of taxes". Obama proposes exclusion for estates up to $3.5 million. If you are married, each of you has the $3.5 million exclusion so the total is $7 million. (You need to consult a tax or estate planning attorney who can create what is known as a "credit shelter trust' to preserve both exemptions.) The top rate thereafter would be 45%. According to Jason Furman, Obama's economic policy director, this plan would fully repeal the estate tax for 99.7% of households. Further, Senator Obama would ask that these changes become permanent.

How can you call Obama a (leftist) liberal when he is proposing tax breaks like this for millionaires? In addition, there are various ways a couple could with even more wealth can reduce or eliminate estate taxes. Planning techniques such as Family Limited Partnerships, the Irrevocable Insurance Trust, Grantor Retain Annuity Trust, Private Foundations and others, make this tax truly a voluntary tax. In the classic book written by University of Florida Law Professors Stephens, Maxwell and Lind, the Estate Tax was called a voluntary tax due to all the techniques one could implement to reduce or eliminate the tax. Each year the University of Miami holds an annual Estate Planning Institute, the largest estate planning institute in the United States, where estate planning attorneys and tax attorneys share the techniques that are used to reduce or eliminate this tax. The University of Miami also has a graduate law program in Estate Planning, the only one in the United States where graduate lawyers can go on for advanced study to receive an LL.M in Estate Planning.

The repeal of the estate tax has been supported by over 80% of the population of the United States because the proponents routinely mislead voters about the impact on the average person, and promote myths about losing the family farm. Those issues were addressed over 20 years ago, and there is no need to lose anything. In fact, this tax was designed to prevent large accumulation of financial wealth in a few select individuals who did nothing other than inherit the funds. Obama's plan is really overly generous to the wealthy. He should insist we go back to the pre-Reagan estate tax, when only $1.2 million was excluded from the Federal Estate Tax.

What this means for the estate planning attorneys is quite clear. If your client does not have more than $10 million, there is no reason to create sophisticated estate plans to avoid the tax. Well, there goes the reason to have estate planning attorneys.

What does this mean to individual states? Your state revenues may go down. In the past, up to 16% of the amount collected by the Federal Government could end up in your state coffers. This tax supported schools, roads, and bridges in local communities. Some states were so dependent on this revenue that they created their own separate tax (such as Washington State) to collect funds for deceased individuals who have estates less than $3.5 million. Florida has a Constitutional provision that prohibits the collection of any additional estate tax (no wonder why their public school system is so poor). Florida also cannot impose a personal income tax. (No wonder why Florida's real estate taxes are so high). Each individual needs to consult with their tax advisor regarding the "State Estate tax" in their individual state.

The Republicans Estate Tax Plan

There are 541,000 individuals in the United States who have more than $10 million. They should not have to pay taxes? The republicans will not be bested by a Democrat. He proposes to raise the exemption to $5 million per person; which would mean estates up to $10 million will not have to be burdened with paying taxes on their accumulated assets. If the estate is over $10 million, the tax rate should be only 15%. Mr. Holtz-Eakin, the senator's senior policy adviser and a former director of the Congressional Budget Office says, ". . . this plan should go into place ASAP after he is elected".

Yes a priority indeed! Why should we burden the rich with taxes? How dare we tax rich individuals or even worse their children who did nothing to earn these funds? Who would want to stop the joy of inheriting millions of dollars without having to lift a finger as the tax burden is passed to the working wage slaves of the United States. When I worked as an Estate Planning Attorney in Florida for 15 years, this would be a typical conversation.

"Oh waiter, please fill my cup of coffee, I just inherited $7 million and was sweating whether I had to pay any taxes! I discovered, much to my delight, that I owed none, here is your tip. Make sure part of that goes to the U.S. Government to reduce the horrible national debt." By the way, the IRS is looking closely at that tip money to make sure you pay it to the government. Well I am off to tennis, and then golf. I was going to an estate planning seminar to make sure my children also did not have to pay taxes on this $10 million, but now I will have more time to improve my golf game. I do have to be concerned about income taxes, however since the bulk of my wealth is in stocks and real estate, not much of a concern. I pay no federal taxes on my $3 million in real estate while it appreciates. I have another $2 million in tax-free municipal bonds, which gives me about $100,000 a year tax free to spend. I have $2 million in stocks which I pay pesky capital gains tax on the earnings, which is about $200,000@15% or $30,000. This is annoying. Is there any way we can reduce this pesky capital gains tax? What a burden this year I had to pay $30,000 in taxes! That's a lot of money!"

My violins went out to these people as they were crushed by the weight of their $30,000 tax bill on their $10 million dollar estates. This conversation, though imagined had its genesis in conversations with affluent heirs over many years. The sentiments are not atypical. In Florida, a large majority of the 541,000 households with estates over $10 million claim domicile there because of the low state taxes. In many cases they will own a home in Florida and a home in New York or New Jersey (they will live in Boca and Palm Beach and claim Florida as their domicile). Others will have homes in Ohio and Michigan and claim domicile in Naples and Ft. Myers. Under either plan, they are safe from the burden of estate taxes. If they have an estate larger than this, which many of my clients did, other plans are available to lift the estate tax away from their children. Life Insurance Trust has no cap. You can purchase $10 million life insurance policies by gifting the assets to a trust and the face amount will pass estate and income tax free to your beneficiaries. You can create Family Limited Partnerships and artificially reduce the size of your estate that would be subject to tax. People without any estate would love to have such burdens.

BOTTON LINE: IF YOU ARE DEAD - YOU SHOULD VOTE FOR THE REPUBLICANS. (Of course dead people cannot vote except in Chicago)

"I am only an average man, but, by George, I work harder at it than the average man."

Theodore Roosevelt

THE FEDERAL GIFT TAX

Another tax to stop wealthy individuals from paying taxes before they die is they give away their estates before they die. However, there is a Federal Gift Tax. Prior to the Bush administration, the Federal Estate Tax and Gift Tax were unified. Today, the Gift Tax is separate from the Estate Tax. There are two types of gifts. One is your "lifetime exemption". The other is your "annual exclusion". The Lifetime exemption amounts to about $1 million per individual or $2 million for a married couple. The annual exclusion is about $12,000 per year, per individual. If you go over these amounts, you will have to pay a "gift tax" to the Federal Government. There are additional exclusions for education and health expense. Assets that are given to your children are not taxable unless they exceed the annual exclusion! A family member could receive $24,000 per year income and gift tax free each year from wealthy parents. Now if you WORK for this money you would owe Social Security taxes, plus federal income taxes, plus state income taxes (in most states), plus Medicare taxes. Once again, the law continues the tax policy of not taxing wealthy individuals, while taxing the working class.

BOTTOM LINE: IF YOU ARE RECEIVING GIFTS FROM YOUR RICH PARENTS OR GRANDPARENTS - YOU SHOULD VOTE FOR THE REPUBLICANS.

"There is nothing either good or bad, but thinking makes it so."

William Shakespeare
Hamlet – 1600

FAUX MEETING WITH THE CANDIDATES

The retirement problem will get worse, not better, due to simple math. The wealth disparity will also get worse, not better, for the same reasons. Americans today are a "mathematically challenged" group. If this were not true, Las Vegas would not be the fastest growing city in the U.S. Let's look at the personal retirement problems facing some typical clients.

MEETING WITH JOE AND JILL:

FACTS: Now Joe was your "average" Joe with a nest egg of $50,000 for retirement. Joe is 65 years old and wants to double his money for retirement. Joe backs Obama because Obama is going to eliminate income taxes for seniors over 65 that make $50,000 or less.
PLAN: We will invest the money in stocks and bonds and in 10 years we should double his investment to $100,000. With this nest egg we will start withdrawing about 4% each year or $350 a month for retirement. We went over the plan with Joe and his wife; let's see what they had to say.

Joe: $350 a month? I can't retire on that!

Nick: Well Joe, your investments only can support that income, otherwise we may have to invade principal and then you may have nothing when you are in your 90s like your mother.

Joe: What can I do?

Just then the phone rang.

Joe: It's Barack. Just a minute Barack, I am with Nick Paleveda my tax attorney. What??? You want *me* as your vice president.

Joe: Nick - What should I do?

Nick: Hey, man, the government has a great pension, and you need the job.

Joe: Hello, Barack, yes I will take the job!

MEETING WITH BARACK AND MICHELLE

"FACTS": Barack and his wife are two hard working Americans. Barack graduated from law school at 31 and has held various positions in government and private industry. His wife also has held various positions and is also an attorney. After recent book deals and after paying off student loans, they were able to buy a house for $1.65 million with a $650,000 mortgage. They had a net worth of about one million dollars.

Barack: Michelle and I want to retire in about 15 years. This political stuff is wearing and I want to spend more time with my family. Also, I want to work with America's youth to encourage them to complete high school, to serve their communities, to go to graduate school so that this nation has the educated work force we will need to compete in this global economy.

Nick: We looked at your assets and all you have is the equity in your home. We have no assets available for investment or to contribute to your retirement income". Basically Barack, you need a good pension, or you need to sell your home.

He looked at me, as if puzzled.

Barack: Sell my home?

Nick: Yes, if you sell your home and we have $1 million, we may be able to double that in 10 years so you will have $2 million, enough to give you an $80,000 income for life.

Barack: Only $80,000? Michelle and I make $265,000! How can we live on this, and put our kids through college? I won't be able to send my kids to private schools or college.

He seemed surprised.

Barack: I mean, look at these threads (he pointed to his suit) and the haircut, and the Prius, and my charity work.

He seemed a little concerned.

Nick: Well you need a better pension.

Barack: I see.

Just then he picked up the paper and noticed that George Bush's position was becoming vacant.

Barack: How much is the pension for the President of the United States?

Nick: Over $200,000 a year.

Barack: Gotta go.

And off he ran, and he has been running ever since.

MEETING WITH MITT AND CINDY

Mitt and his wife Cindy came in to review their retirement needs. Mitt was already over 65 and qualified for Social Security, and will start receiving Social Security even though he and his wife are worth over $100 million. A little known fact is that even Bill Gates, Sr., and Warren Buffet will receive Social Security; and the single mom waitress who is trying to support two children will be giving 7.65% of her income to these two gentlemen, while her employer contributes an additional 7.65% of her income to Social Security. That money might be useful to her family. Now if she walked up to give it to Bill and Warren, they would be too embarrassed to take it, but that is what they do each time they cash their Social Security checks. They cannot waive the payment. All they can do is send it in as a contribution to paying off the National Debt, or some other charity.

Ironic isn't it, the waitress is supporting Bill Gates and Warren Buffet! What a great example of our twisted values as a nation.

Mitt: I think we are doing Ok. Cindy is worth about $100 million and we have a pre-nup in place. I am concerned about the estate, what should we do?

Remember, Mitt is not an economic expert, that's why he consults with Bain Capital who doesn't like to listen to poor people whine.

Nick: Mitt, we can invest the $100 million and, in 10 years, you and Cindy will have about $200 million.

Mitt: What happens if I die?

Nick: Cindy will receive the $200 million with no estate tax because there is an unlimited deduction for estate taxes between husband and wives.

Mitt: What happens when Cindy dies?

Nick: The first $10 million will be tax free and the remainder taxed at 35%.

Mitt: 35%!!

Mitt was getting angry.

Nick: Yes the kids get $10 million tax free.

Mitt: 35%!!!

Mitt was getting very angry.

Mitt: Those no good left, cult, government grubbing liberals! I will roll over in my grave before they get 35% of everything I have.

Mitt: Yes, that is true. You will be in your grave when your heirs pay the tax.

Mitt: I am going to do something -- reduce the tax to 0 or 15%. How dare they tax us at death...these are...DEATH TAXES!

MEETING WITH SARAH :

Sarah: Well I really haven't looked at planning. I am only 44. I used to be a mayor of a town with 6700 people after defeating Bullwinkle the moose, and then became Governor. Now after being a hockey mom - I'm headin' to the White House! Isn't America wonderful?

Nick: Yes, it is just unbelievable that you are the Vice Presidential candidate.

Sarah: The White House!

Nick: Sarah, you won't be staying in the White house, that home is reserved for the President of the United States.

Sarah: I won't?

Nick: No, the Vice President has a separate official residence. I noticed on your resume you grew up in Alaska and attended college in Idaho. Have you ever been back East?

Sarah: Oh yes, I have been back East!

Nick: Really, where?

Sarah: Well, I have been as far as Western Montana!
I even travelled out of the country when I went to Kuwait to visit the troops. Since I was with the government, I didn't need a passport.

Nick: I see. Well the good news is that if you are elected, you will receive a generous pension from the federal government. If you lose, then you have about 20 years to save for retirement and accumulate enough assets to retire comfortably. I'm sure that you will probably also receive a pension from the State of Alaska. You should be set.

Now these conversations were pure fiction, however many of these comments have come to me from my 25 years in law practice meeting with clients. Unfortunately, in televisions ads and in books, many authors will place fiction before you as if it were fact. Some will even make statements such as, "If Obama gets elected the stock market will collapse"; or "if the republicans gets elected we will have 4 more years of Bush". We will not have four more years of Bush; we will have four years of the republicans continuing Bush's policies. This could be better; or this could be worse. The stock market will not collapse because nothing in Obama's policy proposals will have a negative impact on the economy as a whole. There are risks inherent in any choice.

"Everything should be made simple as possible, but not simpler."

Albert Einstein

FACT v. OPINION

Albert Einstein was one of the greatest theoretical physicists who ever lived. As smart as he was, he also observed that the most complicated area in his life was the federal income tax system. The federal income tax is only one federal tax on earnings or assets. There are Social Security and Medicare taxes; there is the Estate Tax and the Gift Tax. There are federal excise taxes. Until 1913, the entire federal government operated from customs' revenue. (Duties on imported goods) So when they start talking "tax cuts" or "tax increases" be certain you know which tax.

This book contains both fact and opinion, as do most books. The difference is, we will attempt to highlight what is opinion. Many political scientists, especially a particular one with a Ph.D. from Harvard, attempt to mislead the public by stating his opinion as if it were fact. He goes on in many parts of his book to quote newspaper opinions as if they were fact. The media is full of pundits, and "talking heads", non-experts who share their opinions as if they were fact. Many of these people have little or no expertise in the area that they are discussing. Some are celebrities, and statements they make are opinions about subjects they lack the qualifications and knowledge to justify having any opinion. Too much of the material published today in the political area promotes the goals of the publisher at the expense of presenting the truth.

For example: "If capital gains taxes were to increase, we would lose $ 2.4 trillion."

The "we" here are the stock brokers and wire houses who hold the stocks and other assets, and make their money on each and every trade made each day; not the economy in general. The increase in capital gains taxes would result in less short swing purchasing and selling of stock, and create more stability in the marketplace. The holding period used to be two years, with a 50% tax rate. The market experienced ups and downs, but this gave corporations a longer horizon for planning. During the Clinton administration the capital gains tax rate was 28% as opposed to the Bush administration that has a capital gains tax of 15%. I think, one could argue that the lower rate both increased the general volatility we have seen since 2000, and has led to the reduction of many 401(k) s to "201(k) s".

The "facts" here are purely subjective. My personal observation is that clients are less likely to unload their portfolios in a down market due to the high rate of capital gains tax. The inability or unwillingness to unload the stock when it is going down creates stability in the stock in a down market. When the market goes up, the clients are also unwilling to unload the stock because they don't want to pay the higher capital gains tax. The stock brokers lose because they cannot receive commissions for trades that do not occur. The money managers are compensated on the increase in value due to the assets they have under management, so they do not care as long as the market value increases.

There is another myth that high taxes discourage investment, capital formation and the creation of new businesses. To me, this notion is just plain silly. People spend or save, start new businesses because they can. Marjorie and I would survive about two days in any normal business. Well, actually Marjorie did work for PriceWaterhouseCoopers in Los Angeles for two years when they were simply Price Waterhouse and there were eight major public accounting firms. I have been self-employed my entire professional life. The idea of working for someone else is appealing. The reality is that structure is impossible for some of us; and we are usually self-employed, if we are successful.

The venture capitalist will still attempt to raise funds for an IPO regardless of the capital gains tax, if the idea is a worthy one to take to the market. The marginal ideas still go by the wayside; capital formation does not stop regardless of the tax policies. Even during the depths of the Depression, individuals started new businesses. For many of them it seemed the only way to survive. For others, it was something they chose to pursue because they could. Another factor in the creation of new businesses is the working conditions prevalent in the economy as a whole and the ease of entry for any particular individual. There are so many factors in this calculation, that to reduce business creation to depending solely on marginal tax rates is nonsense. So when pundit's state, "raising capital gains will hurt the market by $2.4 trillion" this is all made up. (Of course what I expressed was also my own opinion based upon empirical observation). Facts are facts: such as the tax on SSI and Medicare is 15.3% total. One half is paid by the employer. The other half is paid by the employee. The myth (also known as 'conventional wisdom') is, that this high rate of tax should cause a recession. In reality, the rate has been there since 1990, and we have experienced periods of growth, stagnation, and recession during its lifetime.

The more important question is, "Who is paying the tax?" For most of the history of the federal income tax, the rates on incomes from about $400,000 and up have been between 70% and 90%. We had this completely illogical, "unfair" notion that the wealthy should pay more than those of modest means. As I recall, "Noblesse oblige." – Madame Laura Nichols my sixth grade French teacher. (Marjorie) I was taught that with wealth and education came responsibility to the wider community, especially the "less fortunate". We had the idea that we were in this together, and that everyone needed to do what they could to make the world a

66

better place. I attended a private school in Seattle that later merged with Lakeside School, attended by Bill Gates and Paul Allen. People in this part of the world still mostly live by that value. We still believe in doing our share and helping others. It makes for a pretty nice place to live. More important, the country managed to prosper, people at every level were doing well, except for the very poor, in spite of our "misguided" tax policies.

The other point is that we need to exercise caution when economists present their "theories". From what I have seen over the past 40 years, most of them have a specific social and political agenda behind that policy. They are very good at presenting half-truths as "fact" to support their policy statements. At some point, each one of us has to step back and look at where we were and what worked and then, look at what we need to take care of, and ask the question, "Does this policy help one segment of the country and is this choice going to put us where we intended to be?" The facts are that the Reagan tax policies have been a raving disaster for the middle class, and have been an absolute windfall to the wealthy.

BRANDING—ONE WORD OPINIONS

Some of us remember that in 1976 till 1980 Jimmy Carter did his best to guide us about the problems of using fossil fuels; and what did we do? We elected Ronald Reagan and went in the direction that "felt good" and ignored the energy problem. Carter was "too" honest, he didn't want to "horse trade" with Congress. He was about doing the "right" thing. He was "provincial", "dull", not "with it". We were about being "hip", sophisticated. We trusted the "Great Communicator" and built up huge deficits and an enormous National Debt. Unlike Richard Nixon, Reagan could never balance the budget. In retrospect, who do you think was right?

Marjorie: Now, I just want to preface this chapter with the observation that I voted for Reagan. I believed him. Like Reagan, I have always believed that people need to solve their own problems; that you can't fix what is wrong in their lives for them. I was also relatively young and dumb. By dumb, I don't mean unintelligent. No one would ever accuse me of that. However, I have been ignorant, lacking in experience, the follower of relatively poor role models, pig headed, and unwilling to examine an alternative that doesn't fit my world view, indeed often unwilling to admit that there may be a better alternative than the one I chose.

I attended NYU in a program to obtain a masters degree in English education. The professors at NYU gave us one piece of information that you must know:

"People will reject, out of hand, any information that does not conform to what they already know to be true, regardless of the qualifications of the source of that information."

What this means is that, if you believe that drilling offshore and in ANWAR (Alaska National Wildlife Refuge) is necessary to reduce the price of gasoline at the pump, no amount of factual information to the contrary from experts such as T. Boone Pickens, (this country's patriarch of the oil industry (opinion)), the science community, leading economists in England, Europe, China, and India or any other objective source will affect your belief. You have to be asking for truthful information. You must be willing to verify American oil industry information with independent sources of information. You must verify what the pro-drilling forces are telling you with another responsible information provider not connected to the oil industry. Most of all, you must want a solution to this crisis more than you want to be right. You have to be willing to admit that you may be mistaken in what you believe. You must be willing to change your thinking if the facts do not support what you believe.

Why would you want to do that? It would confront you with the possibility that a most dearly held "truth" is WRONG.

Now we all know that in America, the worst sin is being wrong; especially, if you are wrong about a belief that is central to your local culture. The Republicans have used the factor of cultural history and identity to their advantage for the past 28 years. For a significant portion of the population, cultural and religious traditions trump facts 100% of the time. You could not change their minds if they were on the wrong end of a gun. Firmly planted feet supporting a firmly closed mind unwilling to consider any possibility contrary to TRADITION is a badge of honor; a sign of loyalty to your group, a sign that you are one of the "smart" ones.

That is why people continue to revere George W. Bush, and have elevated Ronald Reagan to sainthood. These are basically "good" people. They obey the laws; they pay their bills; they attend church-at least most Sundays. However, if Christ came to give us repentance to help us grow and become more Christ like, for these people it was wasted effort. They just don't get that aspect of Christianity. It will forever remain beyond their comprehension. If you are mortally offended by this observation, it is because I'm describing you.

"Insanity is doing the same thing over and over and expecting a different result." You will not get yourself out of a situation at the same level of thinking that got you into it.

The most formidable tool used to keep us comfortable in our often erroneous beliefs is THE LABEL.

"What do you do if you're branded and you know you're a man…" Chuck Connors starred in this T.V. series called "The Rifleman" years ago. Today we still have kindergarten level name calling by people with Ph.D.'s from Harvard University. It is amazing in this world of high speed Internet, jet service throughout the world and nanotechnology that Ph.D.'s from Harvard will engage in name calling and branding to influence ignorant Americans into voting for his or her candidate.

He is a "black American". A "mulatto", said one Ph.D. from Harvard in his book Obama Nation. (I have not heard anyone call Tiger Woods a "mulatto"). Perhaps in reality Barrack Obama is the Tiger Woods of Politics. Articulate, intelligent and hard working, he was able to secure the nomination for President from the Democratic Party without stumbling. The same Ph.D. from Harvard, unable to successfully mount an attack on Barack, started labeling Obama's parents, preacher and former associates. Apparently, if your father did this and your mother did that, you are going to do the same thing. Is this thinking logical on any level? For every child who follows the path taken by a parent, there are plenty of us out there who have headed in a completely different direction. Marjorie's mother did not go beyond high school and her father had one quarter left for a BS in mechanical engineering. My mother was a Registered Nurse and did graduate work in nursing in New York City. My father graduated from high school and got his higher education serving in Europe during World War II. He owned his own printing business in Tampa, Florida. My sister, one brother and I graduated from college. I stayed in school to avoid work. When I got my LL.M, there was nowhere else to go and I started my own law practice. Marjorie obtained an accounting degree and obtained a master's in tax from USC. She later finished her English degree at GA State University when we lived in Atlanta. We are perfect illustrations that sometimes they do "fall far from the tree". There are a lot of us.

The purpose of using a label is to make the person who is being labeled into an object. When you are dealing with a person as a person, there are many social constraints affecting how you treat that person. In order to conform, to "feel good" about yourself, you have to treat each individual with respect, courtesy, compassion, as a neighbor, a brother. This country was founded on the idea that governments, above everything else, must be fair. To everyone.

What does treating people well and treating everyone fairly have to do with labels? When you label a person or a group, you cease looking at them as people just like you. They have been reduced to objects. Objects do not have feelings. Objects get in our way. Objects are fair game to manipulate into position without regard for their welfare. Objects act without reason-usually to annoy us or put **us**

69

at a disadvantage. Objects do not suffer. Objects have no "rights". Objects have no valid belief system, needs, thoughts, or feelings. We do not have to consider their humanity. We need not concern ourselves with their circumstances or the effects of our goals on their well-being. We can devalue them; and then, we can ignore them.

Labels are the basis for racism, sexism, fanaticism, and every other form of extremism. For the citizens of a country founded so that all could pursue "life, liberty, and happiness", turning even one person into an object by using a label is the height of hypocrisy. "Christians" who consistently push agendas failing to respect the needs and humanity of those whose values differ from their own have no right to use that sacred name. Using the name of Jesus Christ to justify treating other people as objects is what got us the Holocaust, the Crusades, and the Salem Witch Trials. Any relationship between the words and actions of these people and the example of Jesus Christ during his time among us simply does not exist. These chapters in human history could not be farther from "Christ like" conduct.

Labels have been the basis for slavery, segregation, genocide, the exploitation of women and children, the deprivation of decent working conditions and wages for factory and mill workers, child labor, and other untold reprehensible behavior by those in power. Labels are at the root of most conflicts between human beings in the home, at work, at church, and in the political arena.

We all need to ban the use of labels, and begin looking for long-term solutions to the challenges before us.

In politics, branding is done to make us feel safe and superior, and to represent that the opponent is somehow inferior, lacking in vision, inexperienced, or worst of all, A GREAT RISK.

"Why I am a conservative"-What does that word mean?

"Why I am a liberal"-what does that mean?-We make it up.

"A word means whatever I want it to mean, nothing more or less" said Lewis Carroll in his book, Through the Looking Glass. If we "brand" candidates, we can ignore the issues and not have to think. "I won't vote for Obama because he is a leftist". I guess lower deficits; less debt and lower taxes make you a "leftist".

"I am going to vote for Obama because he is a liberal!" Lower taxes and lower deficits make you a liberal? These terms have been used with so little discrimination as to render them meaningless. Worse yet, their use makes meaningful discussions impossible. Branding is pure lying at its worst.

We like to put people into groups with labels. Labeling is an American pastime. He is "rich". He is "poor". So what? The "what" is the implication that each of us brings to that label. So often, I encounter a situation where someone describes a challenge in terms that make it sound like a disaster when, in reality, one of the parties misinterpreted a communication. The result is that a minor issue becomes a major issue until I finally determine that we simply have a "failure to communicate."

In the political arena, labels remove the necessity to think about the facts presented and the possible solutions. Instead of examining objective facts based on objective research, we run to the information source most closely conforming to our preconceived notion of what the solution most desirable to us will be, and then look for facts to support our position. How can this process possibly lead to an acceptable solution, let alone the optimal solution?

It hasn't for the past thirty years. We are now in the worst economic condition since the Great Depression. The middle class is disappearing; the minimum wage will not support an individual, let alone a family. Two minimum wage earners together cannot support a family. Health insurance is unreachable for a significant portion of the population, whether the number is 44 million or 47 million doesn't matter, if you are one of the uninsured. Children with chronic illnesses rely on the emergency room for primary care. We have created an enormous deficit from a surplus and wages have stagnated, jobs are going overseas, the balance of payments is out of control because we are borrowing money from the Chinese to purchase goods they manufacture burning "our" oil and thus raising our gas prices.

As long as we substitute labels for honestly exploring all the possibilities, either administration will accomplish about as much as the other because we will remain gridlocked.

WE MUST BAN ALL LABELS AND RESERVE THE TERMS "REPUBLICAN" AND "DEMOCRAT" TO INDICATE THE POLITICAL PARTIES.

St Luke Chapters 18 - 23

18 And a certain ruler asked him, saying, Good Master, what shall I do to inherit eternal life?

19. And Jesus said unto him, Why callest thou me good? None is good, save one, that is God.

20. Thou knowest the commandments, Do not commit adultery, Do not kill, Do not steal, Do not bear false witness, Honor thy father and thy mother.

21. And he said, All these I have kept from my youth up.

22. Now when Jesus heard these things, he said unto him. Yet lackest thou one thing: sell all that thou hast, and distribute unto the poor, and thou shalt have treasure in heaven: and come follow me.

23. Now when he heard this, he was very sorrowful: for he was very rich.

WHAT WOULD JESUS DO?

Unfortunately if you say Obama, the "red herring" of ABORTION and GAY MARRIAGES will plague you like locust from the Old Testament. Remember the BIBLE BABY! All the plagues from the Bible will come to haunt you if you vote in your economic interest. Remember the Republican Party is the party of the Christian right, or are they?

The "Christian New Testament" that the "Evangelicals" for lack of a better description, seem unfamiliar with a story found in Mark and in Luke 18:18-23. The so called religious right (and everyone else) want to ignore this area of the New Testament (don't we all). The Reformation was based on the premise that the Popes had so corrupted the teachings of Jesus Christ that they no longer had his authority to represent Him on the earth. Initially, the Lutherans resembled German Catholics, the English resembled English Catholics, and so on. Then the Baptists, Methodists, the Presbyterians and other Protestant churches began to dissent with the more catholic churches, and we were off to the races. Christians today like the "cafeteria approach" to religion. Christianity pretty much means whatever the Evangelicals say it is. While they are obsessed with banning abortion and denying civil rights to homosexual individuals, they ignore issues of dealing humanely with the poor, providing solutions for the social ills that confront us. They seem to forget that we are indeed our brother's keeper.

This story is recounted also in Mark 10:16-20. In many cases this area is being ignored by the so called religious right, or they rationalize their unwillingness to sacrifice personal assets to benefit others. The point is that a high estate tax actually follows Christian philosophy. It serves the purpose of allowing taxpayers to restore assets to the country that has protected them and provided the means to accumulate their wealth. It also serves to keep the playing field level and eliminate the concentration of wealth by fewer and fewer citizens. We did quite well as a nation until 1980 with hefty estate taxes. High estate taxes also serve to encourage charitable giving, fairer wages to workers, and social equity

What would Jesus do? Mike Huckabee was right when he said that Jesus was too smart to run for political office. However, Jesus did make it clear on numerous occasions that accumulating wealth was not in the best interest of one's immortal soul. Today, the system to distribute one's wealth is the federal tax system. The Republicans have been using our tax system to redistribute wealth to the wealthy for the past 28 years. Somehow redistributing wealth is only a bad thing if you take from the rich to meet national responsibilities and give all citizens the opportunity, skills and access to a better life. Where is Robin Hood when you need him?

"One cannot hold a man down in the ditch without remaining down in the ditch with him."

Booker T. Washington

THE OBAMA TAX POLICY

The "New Republicans"-Borrow and Spend!

Looking objectively at the tax policy of Obama v. The republicans, I would say Obama is the more fiscally conservative candidate. Why? The republicans is increasing the National Debt and creating huge deficits, where Obama is also creating more deficits, but not as great as Senator Republicans. The fact is that the greatest deficits were created by Ronald Reagan, George H.W. Bush and George Bush. The National Debt now stands at $9.6 trillion dollars. Most of this problem can be accounted for by the three administrations mentioned above. The Democrats, on the other hand are branded as a "tax and spend", liberal party dedicated to making us a socialist country. Which is better borrow and spend, the "New Republicans" or "tax and spend" like the old Democrats?

The Old Democrats-"Tax and Spend"

The Democratic Party has a history of increasing government programs and raising taxes to pay for these programs. These programs in some cases have been good and some cases have been a disaster. In any event, under the current Obama proposal most people will have LOWER taxes. If you have income under $100,000, your taxes will be LOWER than under the "New Republicans" who will give you HIGHER taxes. So which do you prefer? Most rational people prefer LOWER taxes, however if you do not like the Democrat's middle ground on abortion and "gay rights", you may vote to impose HIGHER taxes on yourself. The majority (?) of Americans voted for higher taxes for the lower and middle classes in the last election. They put a President in office who ignored their demands to start pulling out of Iraq. Now, the surge may have provided some respite in some areas in Iraq, the fact remains that what turned the table were local leaders cooperating with the American troops to rid their towns of the Taliban. We will never know what would have happened if we had not implemented the Surge. After all of the republican wrong calls on Iraq, I am not going to give him a pass on this one. The point is that these labels are preventing us from making rational decisions based on the facts and circumstances. That is no way to run a country.

The elephant in the room is the fact that we are spending $10 billion each month on a war we can't afford because our President refuses to raise taxes to pay for it. Given that we are so dependent on foreign oil, that the Chinese and other not so friendly countries hold much of that debt; this seems pretty stupid. We are paying them interest on top of the debt. Our roads, airports, and bridges are crumbling. The air traffic control system is antiquated and dysfunctional. Our schools are a national disgrace. The Boomer generation is facing retirement knowing they can't retire, and traffic is choking our roads because unlike the rest of the world, we refuse to invest in mass transit. Fixing this would create thousands of good-paying jobs. Investing in alternative energy production, converting automobiles to LNG or CNG like Iran is doing today would provide jobs and eliminate the need for any foreign oil. What are they waiting for? What are you waiting for?

Obama has been leery of being cast as a tax and spend Democrat, hence he proposed tax cuts for most everyone who earns under $100,000 and increased taxes on those who earn over $250,000 to balance the revenue flow. The Tax Center estimates that the Obama plan will increase the National Debt over 10 years by $2.8 trillion. In contrast, the same institute estimates that The republican tax plan will increase the National debt by $4.2 trillion over the next 10 years. The difference of $1.4 trillion is hugely meaningful in terms of our ability to repay these deficits.

Currently the so-called "conservative" Bush administration announced it would run a $482 billion dollar deficit next year. The deficit will be added to the current national debt which is $9.5 trillion. Now a $10 trillion increase in the National Debt is the legacy of the fiscally conservative Republicans? What are you smoking?

Several government agencies including the Government Accountability Office (GAO), the Congressional Budget Office, the Office of Management and Budget (OMB) and the U.S. Treasury Department have reported that the federal government is facing a series of critical long-term financing challenges. Expenditures from programs such Social Security, Medicare, and Medicaid are growing faster than the economy overall as the population matures. These agencies warn that spending from Social Security, Medicare and Medicaid and the INTEREST ON THE NATIONAL DEBT, will exceed all revenues collected from taxes. Several individuals have brought this issue to our attention such as David Walker, the former head of the GAO, investment guru Robert Kiyosaki, and billionaire Ross Perot. Unfortunately, Mr. Walker resigned in March of this year. He had undertaken a Fiscal Wake-Up Tour to explain the huge problem we are ignoring, and ran into some heavy opposition from the administration. I'm sure his replacement will abandon this effort and toe the party line and misleading the taxpayer.

Before the September 11, 2001 attacks, the Bush administration projected there would be a $1.288 trillion dollar surplus from 2001-2004. In 2005, this was changed to a deficit of $850 billion or a swing of $2.138 trillion. Why? About 49% came from the economic losses during the recovery after the attack, about

29% was self-imposed with the Bush program to reduce taxes for the rich, and 22% was due to War, specifically the made up War in Iraq. Quite frankly 51% of the $2.1 trillion dollar loss was due to George's ideas. We paid him a salary and benefits exceeding $400,000 a year to put us $2.1 trillion in the hole. No private company would ever hire him as a CEO given this track record. Projections between different groups will sometimes differ because they make different assumptions. For example, in August 2003, a CBO report projected a $1.4 trillion deficit from 2004 through 2014.

However, a mid-term and long-term joint analysis by the Center on Budget and Policy Priorities, the Committee for Economic Development, and the Concord Coalition stated that "in projecting deficits, CBO follows mechanical 'baseline rules' that do not allow it to account for the cost of any prospective tax or entitlement legislation, no matter how likely the enactment of such legislation may be". According to this report, this "adjustment" to the CBO's official 10 year projection, replacing the assumptions used with more realistic assumptions about the cost of budget policies, raised the projected deficit to $5 trillion from $1.4 trillion.

In the current scheme of fiat money, the U.S. Government is free to print all the money it wants. Consequently, the government cannot technically go bankrupt. Unlike you and me, when they run out of cash, they just print some more! What a fun idea! The only trouble is that historically, printing money on that scale leads to hyperinflation and sinks the value of the Dollar like a rock.

Under the current monetary system, any debtor nation can simply print money. The ability to print money does not negate the fact that Russia did default on its bonds, and several U.S. cities have declared bankruptcy. (See When Genius failed-the story of Long Term Capital Management)

"Politics is supposed to be the second oldest profession. I have come to realize that it bears a very close resemblance to the first."

Ronald Reagan – Remarks at a business conference
Los Angeles – 1977

THE REPUBLICAN TAX POLICY

The Republican tax plan is also to lower taxes, more for the upper class and less for the average wage earner. Does this sound familiar? He also plans to reduce taxes on capital gains and reduce Estate Taxes. Who benefits from lowering these taxes? Not you and me. Those who benefit are the same folks who benefited under the Bush Administration. You guessed it--the rich benefit from these policies. And what about our responsibility as a nation to pay our bills?

What are you some left-wing liberal, risky Democrat? See how useful labels can be? As soon as you view people proposing a solution that will require everyone to share some pain, they are RAISING TAXES. Well, I think raising taxes in the present situation is perhaps-dare I say it?-appropriate.

If you think John's tax program is free of risk, I hope you are prepared to lose everything you own, and saddle your children and grandchildren with debts they did nothing to acquire on money that was borrowed from countries who don't like us very much so that the rich and famous would have lower tax rates. Everything The republicans is proposing results in a larger Federal deficit than Obama's plan. These policies result in a greater national debt than under Obama. Is the republicans really fiscally conservative?

The argument for lower capital gains taxes is that more taxes are collected if the rates were or are lower. Why? The cost of exchanging properties is now lower enticing more activity in the market of trading properties such as stock bonds and real estate. Does this create more wealth? Let's take a look at a micro example. If you have a property worth $500,000 and you sell it (because it appreciated in this example from $0) you would owe $75,000 in capital gains taxes under theThe republicans proposal. Next you take your gains and you purchase other properties worth $425,000. Someone else owns the $500,000 property.

How did this produce more goods? It did not. How did it produce more services? Well, lawyers and brokers get paid on assisting to complete the transaction. How does this increase "capital formation"? It does not. If you believe the argument that lower capital gains tax rates increase tax revenues, you probably would like some swamp land I know about in Florida.

In addition, Section 1031 of the IRC allows real estate to be traded on a tax free basis. There also exists 368(a)1(B) of the IRC that allows your stock to be exchanged tax free for stock of another company.

So what does it mean? If you increase the capital gains tax, and the tax cost to sell the property is $120,000 or 30% rather than 15%, the property owner would be more likely not to trade the property. So revenue from Capital Gains taxes will drop. However, have they taken into account that if you double the rate, you only need half the trades? The argument is less activity will result in lower revenue from capital gains taxes collected.

However, if you are an executive in a company or stockholder who would like more stability in the stock, this would cut down on excessive trading to reap short term gains. When executives and money managers can plan with longer horizons for their decisions and think long term, the decision making becomes better and the market increases in value. Hence, during the Clinton administration we saw 28% tax on capital gains and a bull market at the same time. Arguably, the reduced volatility in the market would contribute to greater value increases, providing greater tax revenue over time.

Further, this assumption provides no possibility for other tax adjustments to provide for more revenue from other sources. This kind of closed thinking without considering obvious alternatives is a favorite ploy of those opposed to reforming anything. Why would they want reform? The system works splendidly if you have an income in excess of $350,000 or a net worth in excess of $7.5 million.

"If we make up our minds that this is a drab and purposeless universe, it will be that, and nothing else. On the other hand, we believe that the world is ours, and that the sun and the moon hand in the sky for our delight, there will be joy because the artist in our soul glorifies creation."

Helen Keller

WHO SHOULD YOU VOTE FOR?

Voting is a personal choice. Everyone is in a different situation financially and philosophically. If you look at the pure, short-term economics, the choice is clear. If you earn less than $100,000 you should vote for Obama. If you earn more than $250,000 you should vote for the republicans. If you earn between $100,000 and $250,000, you should vote for the candidate based upon your personal values and vision for America. In any event, whoever you vote for will have increasing challenges on the financial front. A growing National Debt, increasing deficits, and an aging population will make higher taxes an unavoidable reality. The aging population will put more strain on government programs such as Medicaid, Medicare and Social Security. The sooner we accept that and raise our taxes to meet those obligations, the less painful it will be for everyone.

Who ate my cheese?

WHO ATE MY CHEESE?

A National bestselling book came out with less than 100 pages called, *"Who Moved My Cheese?"* Many have read this book, and understand the similarities to their lives. In the meantime, the tax code has been rewritten to add another chapter: *"Who **ate** my cheese."* Most people are unaware that the "cheese" has been eaten by 1% of the population. I like to call them the 3d standard deviation, which represents about 1% of the population or 3 million individuals in the United States. These people are just like the rest of us. Some of them are responsible, hard-working contributors to society. Some are lazy, unscrupulous reprobates. A lot are in the middle. What they have contributed to warrant the astronomical rewards they have received is not exactly clear. What is clear is that their overwhelming wealth should be advantage enough. There is no reason to reduce their taxes in the face of mounting deficits, and a looming retirement crisis. They control almost 40% of the assets in this country. The lowest 40% control about .2% of the assets in this country. Labor is the backbone of the American economy, if you break the backbone, the rest of the body doesn't work. You can only put so much weight on your backbone, and then it will break.

CURRENT WEALTH DISTRIBUTION

It's great to be an American! It's great to be in America! America is the land of opportunity. This is a land where you can own one home like Barack Obama; or you can own two, or three, or SEVEN, like The republicans. Yes, seven homes! You can be in the bottom 40% of Americans and own....well.......nothing. Not really, you still have one vote, just like the top 1% except other issues may stop you from acting in your own best interest such as, Gay rights, Gun rights, Abortion, Family Values and any other hard core beliefs which keep you in poverty. Most of you cannot afford to buy this book, have no money for education because you have nothing, nothing except the power to vote. If wealth were distributed more equally, then we would have what is called "equality". Others may call this "extreme leftist policies". It should be empirically obvious that when you work 15.3% of your earnings are IMMEDIATELY removed for payroll taxes. When multimillionaire passes $7 million to his children, there are no taxes. When a multimillionaire gives $24,000 to his children, there are no taxes, and when a hedge fund manager earns millions, he may pay taxes at 15.0%-YOU will pay more in payroll taxes! Is this a good policy for America? In some countries, such as England, while they like their royals, they have created a prosperous, vibrant economy, and still provided national health care, university is available for the cost of room and board, and they take care of the poor.

Tax laws should be fair. Today, the system is upside down and in many cases favors the wealthy over the poor. Any thoughts of change are countered with labels such as "You are an extreme leftist with a cult of personality". Our current system enriches the wealthy at the expense of the poor and middle class. The Congressional Budget Office, the General Accounting Office, the Census Bureau, the Comptroller General, have all reported on the widening gap in income and wealth slowly destroying the social connections that are the fabric of America. The obsession with celebrity, the growing excesses in compensation to executives, sports figures, entertainers, and others is slowly eroding the principals of love of country, service, fairness, respect for the law, for government, for one another. We have lost our commitment to leaving this world a better place for our children and grandchildren. We have lost our commitment to honor our families and serve our communities. Rugged individualism has been replaced with self-centered, winner-take-all greed. When I began my career, executives recognized that their employees were part of a team. Now, self absorbed CEOs have convinced themselves and their boards that the value of that executive for one year's work exceeds the payouts from the lottery. What kind of warped thinking would lead to that absurd conclusion?

We are at a crossroads in our history. We have been carefully misled to our precarious place in the global community by a cynical, calculating, manipulative political party because they told us what we wanted to hear. They used labels, their own urban myths, obfuscation, dissembling and prevarication to further their agenda. We were too busy, too ignorant, too unwilling to explore other possibilities to notice. We let them ship our jobs overseas to increase their ever-increasing wealth without thought about the long-term effect of their conduct or the trust they were betraying. We just sat on our hands and let them.

"She always says, my lord, that facts are like cows. If you look them in the face hard enough they generally run away."

Dorothy L. Sayers, *Clouds of Witness*, 1956

TAXES AND FINANCIAL EDUCATION IN AMERICA

Financial education in the United States is at an all time low. Students are required to take math, English, history and science to graduate from high school. The SAT is generally a measure of only two skills, math and English. Our requirements for financial education, which everyone will face and everyone needs to learn is Zero. That's right Zero, Zilch, and Nada. In order to run your financial life, zero education is required.

Now, we do require drivers' education in order to drive a car. Can you imagine when your teenager is 16, hand him or her keys to the car and say, "Go for it!" with no drivers' education, no one sitting next to him or her, no drivers test! This is what we do now to our youth when they are 18. Here are the keys to your financial life, "Now go for it!" No wonder lives are wrecked with bloated unnecessary student loans, credit cards, and obscene mortgages.

Financial education is practically non-existent in our schools.

High School:

In high school, you can take courses on Algebra, Trig., Calculus, English, Biology, and Chemistry-but in my high school, no Financial Education Courses were offered. There were no retirement planning courses.

College:

In college you can take courses in political science, history, calculus, a wide variety of subjects, but no course in financial education. (There is a "finance course" but it is usually theoretical and quantitative).
There were no retirement planning courses.

The MBA program:

Course work is offered in management, marketing, accounting, economics, finance etc. (Once again a "finance course" but it was theoretical and quantitative, not practical).

Law School:

The course work in Law School consists of: Contracts, Torts, Civil Procedure, Criminal law, Real Property Law etc. There are no courses on financial education or retirement planning.

LL.M Masters of Law in Tax:

The course work in Graduate Law School consists of: Income Tax, Corporate Tax, and Estate Tax, Oil and Gas tax and FINALLY Pensions and Profit Sharing-retirement planning!

Why did it take so long? A course like this should be offered in High School. Retirement planning and financial education is at an all time low at a time when people are on their own when it comes to retirement.

1.   Most people know little about how the stock of Hilton Hotels is performing choosing not to follow the stock, but follow every move of Paris Hilton.

2.   Most people know very little about the ownership and performance of Carnival Cruise Lines but know every line from Tom Cruise.

3.   Most people spend hard earned dollars watching films about James Bond and his performance, but cannot comprehend how a corporate bond works.

Financial education and retirement education would receive an "F" in our public school system as in most cases it is not even offered. If we are to exist in a capitalistic society and compete in a global capitalistic world, we must educate our youth as to how capital works. There are other tests offered which measure little and mean nothing. In Washington, they have the WASL. A test which if you do not pass it, you do not receive your high school diploma. This test is normed only in the state of Washington; hence it has no bearing on how the students stack up against other states-let alone the world.

Warren Buffet stated:
"I made my first investment at age 11. I was wasting my life up until then"-<u>The Tao of Warren Buffet</u>; Scribner Publishers New York 2006.

"You are moving into the most competitive age the world has ever known. All around you is competition...sacrifice anything that is needed to be sacrificed to qualify yourselves to the work of the world...and your wealth will increase as you gain education and proficiency in your chosen field."-Gordon B. Hinckley-
<u>Way to Be</u>; Simon and Schuster (2002)

Iowa also has its test ITBS, some students call the test. These tests don't prove anything. Florida has a "literacy test" which if you fail it; you cannot receive a high school diploma. One student I have personal knowledge failed the test. He received a 1580 on the SAT and later went to Harvard undergraduate and Harvard law school. (He did retake the test and passed it).

"At 83 Thomas Edison was still intensively active as ever, and when it was proposed to relieve him of deafness, he declined, saying that his infirmity helped him to think, and, I want to do a lot more thinking before I die."

Gamalileil Bradford – National Business

THE RETIREMENT CRISIS

This is an area not addressed by any politician because this problem will dwarf the National Debt, and there are no solutions that anyone will like. The best we could hope for is that the electorate will suck it up and actually agree to pay for the heedless reckless spending spree of the last 50 years.

Here is the basic problem. The average income today is around $45,000 per year. The population is aging rapidly, and more people are looking forward to retirement. The lump sum amount needed to replace the $45,000 per year is about $900,000. The average savings for an American is $50,000. This means that the average American is only $850,000 short to replace her income at retirement. This is not a concession to equal time; however, this issue falls unduly on women, who have not received equal pay for equal work.

The retirement problem is different for different people. If you have saved the necessary funds, no need for concern. If you want a greater than $45,000 income, you will need to save more. The amount you need to save is an individual choice. If you are use to a $90,000 per year lifestyle, you will need about $1.8 million to retire comfortably. If you need an income of $135,000 you will need about $2,700,000, and if you need an income of $180,000 you will need $3,600,000. All these numbers will change based on your age, your spouse's age, and can vary; but you get the point. You will need a lot more money than you have to meet your retirement goals. You should figure (based on the low interest rate environment) that you can withdraw about 5% of your funds each year for retirement. This problem can be helped if you have a pension, or draw on Social Security. The problem is Social Security may cover up to around $20,000 of your $45,000 annual income needs. Social Security also has problems of its own which is beyond the scope of this book. Depending on Social Security at the current benefit levels is risky.

How can you save enough for retirement? There are several plans that allow you to save funds on an income tax deductible basis. The problem is that you must begin saving in your twenties. Somehow this is not a value instilled in our young people. Heck, most adult Americans don't understand saving for retirement. Here is a list of tax-favored vehicles to save for retirement.

IRAs	SEPs
401(k) s	SIMPLE IRA, SIMPLE 401(k)
Profit Sharing Plans	Roth IRA, Roth 401(k)
Defined Benefit Plans	
Fully insured Defined Benefit Plans	

Each of these plans may be adopted by you as an individual or as a sole proprietor.

Each one of these plans is riddled with rules and literally thousands of pages of regulations. All have maximum contribution amounts such as:

IRAs-limited to $5,000.00
401(k) s limited to $17,000.00
Defined Benefit Plans limited to lifetime income of $200,000/per year.
Fully insured Defined Benefit Plan limited to lifetime income guaranteed of $200,000/per year. There are, of course, more plans than those mentioned above. There are 403(b) plans, 457 plans, SARSEPS, etc, etc.

"We're a people of rainbow hues and multiple faiths. If that heritage has taught us nothing else by now, it should have taught us this: It's ignorant to think you can judge a man's soul by looking at his face".

Leonard Pitts, - The Miami Herald (Miami), 2001

THE NINE NATIONS OF NORTH AMERICA

Joel Garreau wrote a thought provoking analysis of the cultural centers of North America that included our neighbors to the north and south, because in many ways the regions are so diverse, and yet at the same time, we have come to share much between us. Nick borrowed from the structure and offers this analysis based on our experiences over the past 25 years.

1. The East Coast: The real capital is New York. People from the east coast talk faster, move faster and are more financially savvy than their counterparts elsewhere. The homes are more expensive and a nice car is a Mercedes. Three of the largest Airports surround New York: Kennedy, LaGuardia and Newark, NJ. The West is anything past New Jersey and travel is generally limited to Florida and Cruise ships. The schools to attend are found in the Ivy League or Big East and small private colleges spread along the Eastern Seaboard.

2. The Midwest: The real capital is Chicago. People from the Midwest move deliberately and are keen on manufacturing. The breadbasket and the industrial basket of the United States are located here. The homes are less expensive and a nice car is a Cadillac. One of the world's largest airports is in Chicago, O'Hare. West is anything past the Mississippi and vacation spots are the **west** coast of Florida, and Arizona. The schools to attend are the Big 10 and Mid Atlantic Conference.

3. The South: The real capital is Atlanta. Atlanta is the birthplace of civilization as we know it. Witness CNN, known throughout the world and brought to you from Atlanta. The world's largest airport is in Atlanta, Hartsfield. A nice car is a Ford 350 pickup truck, and homes are reasonably priced. Vacation spots include the panhandle of Florida or Branson Missouri. The schools to attend are the SEC and ACC schools.

4. The West: The real Capital is Denver, Dallas and Salt Lake City. Dallas is headquarters to America's team, the Dallas Cowboys. Salt Lake City is headquarters to a 10 million member Church of Jesus Christ of Latter-Day Saints, and Denver is headquarters for everything else. The largest airport land wise is in Denver and Dallas is not far behind. Salt Lake City hosted the 2002 winter Olympics, and a nice car is the Land Rover, as the west has a lot of land to rove. The schools are the Big 12 , the Mountain West, and the WAC.

5. California: The real capital is Los Angeles. Los Angeles is the headquarters of America's talent, TV, motion pictures etc. (Just don't tell

that to anyone in New York or British Columbia) California itself is the worlds 9th largest economy. The homes are expensive as talented people bid up the real estate in the area. A nice car is a Maserati and the homes are very expensive. The schools are the PAC 10.

6. The Pacific Northwest: The real capital is Seattle. This is the land of Microsoft, Amazon and Starbucks. The people of the Pacific Northwest consider themselves to be more tech-savvy than their counterparts around the U.S. A nice car is a Volvo, and the homes can be expensive. The schools to attend are PAC 10 schools. They have their version of fashionable dress: Bermuda shorts, sandals with socks, plaid shirt and ski jacket, knit hat, usually seen around mid-January, when the rest of the world is bundles up sensibly.

7. Alaska and Hawaii; these states are far removed from the "Lower 48". Anchorage is as far from Seattle as San Francisco. In Hawaii we are referred to as Haoles and where we live is the "mainland". Alaska's real capital is Anchorage as Alaska is huge and remote. (The official capital is Juneau.) The people pride themselves on being able to survive the rugged winters. The nice car is a floatplane and the schools are anyone you can get into that is warm. Hawaii is warm and the real capital is Honolulu. Hawaiians pride themselves on an international outlook as they are a stopover for the Asian countries that come to America and the Americans who go to Asian countries. A nice car is one that is fuel efficient.

8. Canada: The real capital of Canada is Ottawa. Honest. Quebec seems to have conceded its place as a mere province, finally. The Canadians are having difficulty choosing a government right now. They have a national health care system that seems to work better in places where the demand is less; and they keep complaining rather than fixing it. They pay higher taxes, have better schools, have kept college costs inexpensive by U.S. standards, and refer to the U.S. as "down south". They play hockey, (talk about a nation of hockey moms) are considerate enough to speak our language; and now that our dollar has sunk we see a lot more of them. Right now they are a much needed shot in the arm for Whatcom County, Washington where we live. By the way, they come in fleets of cars to shop at Costco and buy our "cheap" gas. The Canadian Costco across the border is more expensive. Must be the GST.

9. Mexico: The real capital is El Paso. Mexico City is for the rest of Mexico. They have penetrated virtually every corner of the U.S., unlike the Canadians who are polite enough to go home most of the time. Still, Mexicans provide much needed less expensive labor to keep U.S. workers from seeking higher wages and better working conditions. They

speak Spanish and think that we should too. They are generally lovely, wonderful people who just want nice lives and good educations for their children, who happen to be really cute. There is the gang problem, but we seem to be getting that under control. They want to come here and work. This is good because we need more people to work and pay into our Social Security Trust Fund, as long as they go home and don't actually want their benefits. We need that. We like to vacation on their beaches. They want to work. We should be able to figure this one out; you would think. The Social Security issue is part of the reason the Administration has been so reluctant to actually enforce our immigration laws and protect our borders. Let's see: lower taxes for the wealthy, lower wages for employers to pay, no payroll tax. I can see where the rich think this is a good thing. Once again, greed trumps national economic considerations and national security.

The diversity of culture, values, economic concerns, wealth among these "nations" never ends. How the seven regions in the U.S. stay together under one flag is a daily miracle. It is a miracle that will not continue as long as we do not remind ourselves daily that WE are the government, and that each of us needs to treat the rest of us the way each of us wants to be treated. It is not a socialist notion that the rich should pay the largest share of their income in taxes. Even Warren Buffet noted that:

"But I was lucky enough to be born in a time and place where society values my talent, and gave me a good education to develop that talent, and set up the laws and the financial system to let me do what I love doing---and make a lot of money doing it. The least I can do is help pay for all that."

Barack Obama goes on in his book, *The Audacity of Hope* to note that Mr. Buffet's views are not some soft-hearted sentiment but,

". . . Rather, they reflect an understanding that how well we respond to globalization won't be just a matter of identifying the right policies. It will also have to do with a change in spirit, a willingness to put our common interests and the interests of future generations ahead of short-term expediency"

Since the Reagan administration, the wealthiest of us have grown astronomically wealthier, and the income gap has become the Grand Canyon. It would seem appropriate that the people who benefitted by policies that turned into legalized theft would now make restitution. The Republicans have been redistributing wealth in this country since 1980. I fail to see where reversing the trend is either unfair or "socialist". Reversing the trend is a simple acknowledgement that those policies were a mistake that this nation could not afford. This truly is the time to put country first.

THE OBAMA NATION- A TOME
BY JEROME CORSI, PHD

"COUNSEL'S PERSISTENT AND DELIBERATE EFFORTS TO INCITE PASSION AND PREJUDICE DISTINGUISH THIS CASE FROM THOSE IN WHICH INFLAMMATORY REMARKS WERE FLEETING AND UNINTENTIONAL...COUNSEL HAS BEEN ADMONISHED IN TWO PUBLISHED COURT OF APPEALS OPINIONS SINCE THIS TRIAL BEGAN FOR PRECISELY THE SAME SORT OF HYPERBOLIC AND VITRIOLIC ARGUMENT HE MADE...OVERREACHING, PREJUDICE-BAITING RHETORIC APPEARS TO BE A CALCULATED, ROUTINE FEATURE OF COUNSELS TRIAL STRATEGY. THIS DELIBERATE USE OF IMPROPER ARGUMENT, COUPLED WITH THE ASTONISHING EXCESSIVE VERDICT RENDERED AGAINST DEFENDANT, PRECLUDES US FROM CONCLUDING THAT COUNSEL'S MISCONDUT WAS "INNOCUOUS" AND UNINTENDED"-
GILBERT V. DAIMLER CHRYSLER 685 N.W. 391 (Mich. 2004) Judge Robert P. Young Jr. for the majority.

In court, attorneys are admonished for writing like Jerome Corsi. In the Court of public opinion, you can write these books and even make it to #1 on The New York Times bestseller list (incorrectly marked as non-fiction). Jerome is an inspiration to me. If this clown can be #1 on The New York Times Bestseller list, then anyone can make it. The book is full of hyperbolic and vitriolic language coupled with overreaching, prejudice-bating rhetoric. He claims to be a "political scientist" but there is nothing scientific about his book. The cover itself is amusing: "Leftist Politics and the Cult of Personality". Since when does "personality" become a "cult"? (Are you sure you have a PhD?) Another part of the inside cover says, "Scrupulously sourced with more than 600 footnotes". Footnotes do not equal facts. (Are you sure the NY times made this #1 in Non-fiction?) You can have footnote after footnote which references fiction or made up facts. In fact, no court can take "judicial notice" of a "footnote" as if it were fact. The "footnote" must have an independent basis for fact.

In his book, Mr. Corsi, (or should I say Dr. Corsi?) stated "An Obama presidency would be a repeat of the failed extremist policies that have characterized and plagued the Democratic politics since the late 1960s".

Huh? Bill Clinton expanded the wallets of everyday Americans AND balanced the budget in 1996-the last and only President to do so since Richard Nixon in 1972.

Mr. Clinton was a Democrat.

Mr. Corsi get your facts right.

Ronald Reagan, George H.W Bush, Gerald Ford, and George Bush all ran up huge deficits, by some accounts running up 80% of our National Debt. Reagan, Bush I, and Bush II were Republicans.

Mr. Corsi get your facts right.

According to Jerome R. Corsi, PhD: "After an Obama presidency, we would be a militarily weakened and economically diminished nation." This conclusion was reached by Mr. Corsi PhD after he analyzed the candidates' tax plans. However, the facts do not support his conclusion. Under theThe republicans plan, the National Debt increases at least $1.2 trillion dollars more than under the Obama plan.

Mr. Corsi get your facts right.

Perhaps Mr. Corsi, PhD, believes an increase in the national debt will make this country stronger. Mr. Corsi, PhD, believes we will be "economically weakened". Why? Perhaps because over 8 years under the Obama plan, the average American could be out of all consumer debt. This cannot be good for America and illustrates Obama's "leftist politics".

Mr. Corsi get your facts right.

 Mr. Corsi PhD's book, <u>The Obama Nation,</u> is humorous to anyone who has an IQ over 100. In the preface he states:

"In contrast to Hillary Clinton, Barack Obama has not been vetted, not even by the democrats. Even today he is largely an unknown to all but a handful of dogged political professionals and a concentrated core of political junkies who inhabit Internet (sic) blogs."

I wonder what he thinks of Sarah Palin.

So who does Mr. Corsi PhD support for president? He tells us!

"I have never been a registered member of the Republican or Democratic Party, unless voting in some particular state primary over the past forty years necessitated that result. The only political party I ever consciously joined is the Constitution Party, of which I am a registered member in the State of New Jersey, where I currently reside. . . . I intend to vote in 2008 for Chuck Baldwin, the presidential candidate of the Constitution Party . . ."

WOW! Some serious vetting is going on here! Obviously, Mr. Corsi PhD vetted his candidate well! I am sure the Constitution candidate went through extensive vetting, questioning and enormous scrutiny as never seen before by the American public. The book is obviously fiction and belongs on a different list. I did buy this book, and now, I am left with only one question:

Can I get my money back?

"Posterity is the world to come;

the world for whom we hold our ideals,

from whom we have borrowed our planet,

and to whom we bear sacred responsibility."

Bill Clinton – *First Inaugural Address
(Washington DC) - 1993*

CONCLUSION

If Americans remain ignorant about Taxes, Retirement and Finances, it will be difficult to address the problems we face, let alone solve them. If we are going to be successful in a Global Capital environment, we must understand capital. We must understand taxes, finances and retirement issues. We have the opportunity to turn this ship of state around and set a new course to a brighter future where all will prosper, and the roads, bridges, transportation, and energy policies will work for all of us. We have the opportunity to once again set the example; to not be a shameful excuse for a world citizen. We have the opportunity to act with integrity, to face our challenges with courage to do what is right, to treat our fellow Americans with respect and compassion.

The two plans offer two very different visions for American. This nation grew in stature, prosperity and in power on several powerful principles that we need to rediscover. The first was liberty. The freedom to choose your path, choose your religious beliefs, the freedom from tyranny, strife, persecution, and violence. The next was honor: the duty to God and your fellow man to always act with impeccable integrity, to keep your promises, and tell the truth. The third was a pledge of shared financial responsibility for achieving national goals. In the "Declaration of Independence" the signers declared on our behalf:

"And for the support of this Declaration, with a firm reliance on the protection of Divine Providence, we mutually pledge to each other our Lives, our Fortunes, and our sacred Honor."

Many of them gave their lives and their possessions in sustaining their honor. If you read "the rest of the story" for many of them, they did indeed sacrifice everything. Even Thomas Jefferson died deeply in debt. True, some of that was due to his insatiable curiosity; still, his books replenished the Library of Congress after the War of 1812.

The country expanded with perhaps the most amazing mass migration in all of human history. For every scalawag and outlaw who victimized those pioneers on their way west, first to Illinois and the length of the Mississippi, and then to the West, there are countless tales of men and women sacrificing all they had and pulling together to make better lives for themselves and their children. There are countless tales of neighbor helping neighbor, barn raisings, quilting bees, and celebrations. The University of Washington was established in Seattle because of the vision and dedication of the Denny brothers, who donated the land and then built the first buildings, and hired the first faculty. They had to get all that done before the next meeting of the state legislature, so that the university would be established in Seattle. Today that land is arguably the most valuable commercial property in Seattle, and the university occupies a beautiful ridge going down to Lake Washington. The site was originally used for the Alaska-Yukon-Pacific Exposition of 1909. Husky Stadium sits on the lake and people can get to the games in their boats. Americans would be nothing without imagination, ingenuity, and a sense of humor. We get things done.

During the Great Depression, those with more helped those with less. My mother's family was insulated from the financial impact of that American trial, and my mother talks about men coming to the kitchen door and asking for work. They always left with food and encouragement. In Skagit County, they took measures to see that people got along in ways that allowed them their dignity. Franklin Delano Roosevelt created programs to improve our parks, build dams, bridges, and whatever else was needed. Grand Coulee Dam, the bridge in Whatcom Falls Park, and bridges and park facilities were built by Americans who needed jobs and were willing to work. Dams all over the country made electricity affordable and available. The dams provided much needed irrigation and turned Eastern Washington from a dry, rather desolate stretch of coulees, rolling hills and wide open spaces into a beautiful, vast garden with productive orchards, vineyards, and endless fields of wheat and soy. We accomplished all this by working together as Americans.

During both world wars, we set our individual pursuits aside and gave our money, our time, and our lives to protect this country and defend our allies in their time of need. During World War II, women worked in factories to build the ships, planes, tanks, jeeps, and guns our GIs needed to protect us. We did not give a second thought to higher taxes or rationing. It was all for the troops, for freedom, to "save the world". Korea brought another test of loyalty to country, and of a relatively new president calling to heel a proud national hero. Harry Truman and Dwight Eisenhower were sons of the Heartland. One led with strength through a difficult and controversial time. The other served to once again bind up the nation's wounds and bring us together. Dwight David Eisenhower saved the world. He had demonstrated incredible strength in leading the allied forces to victory, and awe inspiring patience, wisdom and strength in keeping Patton and Montgomery focused on the Germans and not each other. He presided over some of the most talented, passionate and courageous generals the world has ever seen and kept them going no matter how bleak and grim the circumstances. His calm resolute determination inspired confidence and trust in all who knew him. He is the only President in my lifetime, who had the trust and admiration of this entire nation. People might not have liked everything he did; but they never once questioned his motive. We knew he loved this country above everything else. FDR deserves his place in history for his pragmatic goodness and willingness to create some badly needed social programs to balance the American propensity to "go it alone." Dwight Eisenhower towers over the rest of them for his willingness to respect the party and then do what was best for the country. His last speech was a strong warning against losing the country to the interests of the "military-industrial" complex. He warned against giving too much power to corporations, to "special" interest groups, against a dominant military.

We need to revisit that warning and take stock of who is really running his country. Is it you? Or them? If you are not challenging everything generated by the press, the major networks, including CNN and Fox, then you need to wake up.

The press, the television industry, the "Establishment" are controlled, according to nameless sources, by about 100 people. They promote what benefits them and keeps them powerful. Quite often, this is not in your best interest. You have been supporting them for over thirty years. Are you happy with where we find ourselves?

Every news organization on television is slanting the news presentation in support of one candidate. This is not a obvious bias; it is subtle. They are not calling one party on the misrepresentations they make about the other candidate. They misrepresent what is actually occurring on the campaign trail. They are failing to take a really good look at respective qualifications of each candidate. As I indicated earlier, the "talking heads" are paid to present stories in the light of "company policy". They have completely ignored the massive fiscal crisis looming and failed to report the true impact of the various policies promoted by each party for the past 35 years, at least.

For the love of God, country and your family, I implore you to get the facts, ignore the economists, and ask yourself if you have prospered over the past eight years. Ask yourself if the country is in a better position today than eight years ago. Ask yourself if it will be easier for you to afford a college education for yourself or your children than it was eight years ago.

If The republicans is going to change Washington and change our country to head in a new direction, then he has to do one of two things. Either he must pull a bait and switch on the Republican faithful after the election, or he has to dramatically change his policies before the election. Drilling for more oil in Alaska helps the State of Alaska and the big oil companies, and takes the pressure off of Detroit to improve fuel efficiency. It keeps us dependent on oil. T. Boone Pickens is correct. We need to move away from oil yesterday. Natural gas is available. We have the technology. We can modify the existing infrastructure to support LNG cars. We can get this done in 5-10 years, if I know this country. We did amazing things in World Wars I and II. We put a man on the moon in almost no time. We need to choose a leader who will take us where we need to go; not where we are comfortable; and not leave us where we are now.

We will not get out of this mess with the same thinking that got us into it. In the end this election is not about Barack Obama or The republicans. This election is not about my wife or me. This election is about you and your families; about your dreams, your challenges; your character. You have the opportunity to take responsibility for this country, for your obligations to your community and your family. How you meet these responsibilities will demonstrate what government and what kind of a country you create. The internet makes it very easy to get information from the campaigns. Our government agencies, oddly enough, are a wonderful resource. Most of the numbers and facts came from their reports, papers, and presentations. Enjoy the voyage. God speed; and God bless America.

BIBLIOGRAPHY

Articles

Anonymous, The Distribution of Wealth in America, www.faculty.fairfield.com

Anonymous, Wealth and Asset Ownership, U.S. Census Bureau, August 27, 2008

Barack Obama on Tax Reform, www.ontheissues.com

Center on Budget and Policy Priorities, New CBO Data Show Income Inequality Continues to Widen, January 23, 2007, www.cbpp.org

Congressepedia, Rangel Tax Overhaul Plan, various authors, Nov. 8, 2007.

CNN, Obama on Tax reform, www.ontheissues.org

Convention Q&A: Charles Rangel on Obama's Policies, Biden and Clinton, Wall Street Journal Washington Wire, August 25, 2008.

Datair, Annual Dollar Limits, www.datair.com

Domhoff, William, Wealth, Income and Power, Who rules America.net, September 2005, updated December 2006.

DuPont, Peter, Inconvenient Tax Truths, Wall Street Journal October 30, 2007.

Gates, William, Statement of William Gates Sr., OMB Watch June 12, 2002.

Hasset, Kevin, Rangel's Mother of all Tax Bills is Psycho, Bloomberg.com, October 29, 2007.

Holzer, Jessica, GOP calls Rangel tax plan a gift, Leading in the News, October 26, 2007.

McIntyre, Bob, Congressman Rangel's Tax Bill would make the Tax Code Simpler and Fairer and the Changes are All Paid For, November 2, 2007.

Novack, Robert, Rangel's Tax-the-Rich 'Reform', Washington Post,

September 17, 2007. www.washingtonpost.com

Obama, Barack, Tax Fairness for the Middle Class, Obama for America 2008.

Obama Tax Plan Would Balloon Deficit –Washington Post, August 10, 2008.

Obama vs.The republicans Tax Plans: Obama Saves You More, www.bargaineering.com/articles/obama-vs-Romney-tax-plans-obama-saves-you-more.html, as reported from The New York Times

O'Brian, Soledad, "Black in America", CNN July, 2008.

Sahadi, Jeanne, What They Will do to Your Tax Bill, CNNMoney.com, June 11, 2008.

Stein, Ben, A Familiar Tax Tune, But It's Not Mine, New York Times, August 10, 2008.

Tax Policy Center, An Updated Analysis of the 2008 Presidential Candidates' Tax Plan- July 23, 2008.

Urban-Brookings Institute Tax Policy Center, Major Provisions of theThe republicans and Obama Tax Plans, www.taxpolicycenter.org, 2008.

Villarreal, Pamela, Social Security and Medicare Projections, 2008 National Center for Policy Analysis, April 30, 2008.

Wikipedia, Various, 2008.

Woolf, Edward, "Recent Trends in Household Wealth in the United States: Rising Debt and the Middle Class Squeeze", The Levy Economics Institute of the Bard College and the Department of Economics, New York University, updated June 2007.

The New York Times, various articles and opinion letters informed many aspects of the views presented.

The Wall Street Journal, again various articles and opinions informed many aspects of the views presented.

Books

Buffett, Mary, Clark David, The Tao of Warren Buffett, Scribner, 2006.

CCH, Tax Relief and Reconciliation Act of 2006, Walters Kluwer 2006

CCH, Pension Protection Act of 2006, Walters Kluwer 2006

Conrad, Jessamyn, What You Should Know About Politics, Arcade Publishing, (New York) 2008.

Corsi, Jerome, The Obama Nation, Simon and Schuster, (New York) 2008.

Covey, Stephen, Everyday Greatness, Rutledge Hill Press, (Nashville) 2006.

Covey, Stephen, Living the 7 Habits, The Courage to Change, Fireside (New York) 2000.

Black, Roy, Black's Law, Simon and Schuster, (New York) 1999.

DiNunzio, Mario, Theodore Roosevelt Selected Writings, Penguin 1994.

Garreau, Joel, The Nine Nations of North America, Houghton Mifflin, (Boston) 1981.

Hinckley, Gordon B., Way to Be, Simon & Schuster, 2002.

Johnson, Spencer, Who Moved My Cheese, G. P. Putnam's Sons, (New York) 1998, 2002

Kass, The 2008 Pension Answer Book, Walters Kluwer 2008.

Kohler, Mark, Lawyers are Liars, Life's Plan Publishing (Phoenix) 2007.

Obama, Barack, The Audacity of Hope, Vintage Books, 2008.

Partnow, Elaine Berstein, Great Quotes for All Occasions, Alpha 2008.

Schur, Norman, 2000 Most Challenging and Obscure Words, Galahad Books 2004.

Tesser, Ted, The New Trader's Tax Solution, Wiley, 2002.

The Arbinger Institute, Leadership and Self-Deception, Berrett-Koehler Publishers, Inc., San Francisco, 2000.

Thomas, Kaye, Capital Gains Minimal Taxes, Fairmark Press, 2001.

Ziesenheim, Ken, Understanding ERISA, Marketplace Books, 2002.

Government Reports

Treasury Direct, Historical debt Outstandind200-2007 www.treasurydirect.org

U.S. Department of Treasury Fact Sheet Taxes Economics of Taxation 2008

GAO The Nation's Long Term Fiscal Outlook April 2008 Update, www.gao.gov

GAO, Addressing Fiscal Sustainability and Fixing the Social Security System: Two Challenges facing the Nation, The Honorable David M. Walker Comptroller General of the United States.

GAO, A call for Stewardship, Enhancing the Federal Government's Ability to address Key Fiscal and other 21st Century Challenges, December 20071cOe

IRS.gov

The Congressional Budget Office

The Department of the Treasury

The Federal Reserve Board, "Survey of Consumer Finances"

Political Campaigns

www.barackobama.com

www.johnRomney.com

Images

www.istock.com

Various internet sites with no-copyright materials

ACKNOWLEDGEMENTS

I would like to acknowledge the people who have helped give me ideas and encouragement to write this book. The Tax Community is actually very small, and many of these people have made contributions in ways they do not even realize, but I think should be acknowledged. People make all the difference to your life and these people include:

William Saxbe, my cousin who was the Attorney General of the United States under Richard Nixon and Gerald Ford.

Sheldon Smith J.D. LL.M, my Employee Benefit Professor at the University of Denver; Roy Black author of "Black's Law" and my Professor of Criminal Procedure at the University of Miami; Mark Kohler J.D. CPA author of "Lawyers Are Liars"; Ken Jennings author of "Brainiac" and "Trivia Almanac"; Craig Hampton J.D. LL.M, former Dean at St. Thomas Law School and my former law partner; Frank Murphy CPA, J.D. who first introduced me to employee plans in 1984; La Donna Cody J.D. my former law partner who took care of our firm in 1984; Gerald Levy CPA, J.D. who was kind enough to join us in 1984; Frank Cicarrelli who introduced me to insurance in 1984; Kim Cicarrelli CFP who reinvented estate planning; Ken Guard CFP who remains a good friend after over 20 years; Drew Giovannis CFP, and friend for 30+ years who introduced me to selling as a science; Todd Heckman CFP, MSFS a creative mind in estate planning; Glenn Eisenberg CFP now retired; John Koresko, CPA J.D. who has endless knowledge in Fully insured plans; Steve Toth CLU, a great marketer; Greg Purvis from One America and Steve Dobbe from American National (ANICO) who has endless support for us; Don Noble who has endless seminars on Fully insured plans; Keith Baumgarn QPA, CLU, ChFC, FLMI, CRC, who speaks all over the U.S. on Fully insured plans; George Cicotte J.D. who introduced PTE 84-24 (thanks George); S. Derrin Watson, J.D., who wrote *Who Is the Employer?*; and Blinky the Three-Eyed Fish (whoever you are) for your comments on benefitslink.com and all the actuaries and attorneys who work (toil) in this field.

I wish to thank the staff of Executive Benefits in contributing to this book. Charles Gramp, Enrolled Actuary, our chief actuary, has over 37 year's experience in the pension business, and knows far more about retirement plans than could possibly be covered in this book. Charles worked with pension plans prior to the passage of ERISA in 1974. John Bremer, our director of administration, Enrolled Actuary and CPA, has over 35 years in the pension business. Priscilla Habig is responsible for design, (she is from South Africa).

Marjorie Ewing, my editor and spouse, received her Masters in Business Taxation from the University of Southern California and a degree in English from Georgia State University.

113

Also, I would like to acknowledge Peter Pearce who heads up Underwriting and Andrew Magis and Tony Fantini. Finally, without the ups and downs of dealing with clients and producers we would not be able to create great retirement plans. Also thank you John Logan CPA for your endless support.

I also want to thank the IRS, which is a great source of valuable information. The officials I have met at industry meetings are there to help taxpayers to comply with the law: both the spirit of the law and the intent of the law. The service they provide is vital. The IRS is in a constant battle to stop the violators and scofflaws. Without the officials at the IRS, tax laws would be in chaos. We need them to keep plans in compliance and to provide rulings and guidance in certain areas where the law is not clear. You can reach many of the top people by telephone. They attend meetings throughout the country several times each year. Their pronouncements are readily available. We are very grateful for their support and accessibility. If you have questions or comments please e-mail me at nick@ebdgonline.com –Also thanks to Cody Barton and Dan Tucker for their IT support! (plus Debra Royal and Patty Johnson for helping our clients-and David Koenig wherever you are!)

ABOUT THE AUTHOR

Nick Paleveda received his B.A. and M.B.A. degrees from the University of South Florida in 1979. Mr. Paleveda attended the University of Miami receiving his law degree in 1982. Next, Mr. Paleveda attended the University of Denver and received his Master of Laws in Taxation in 1983. He was inspired to go to law school by his cousin William Saxbe, the Attorney General of the United States under Richard Nixon and Gerald Ford. During summers, Mr. Paleveda attended programs in Oxford University for law in England and Harvard University in the U.S. In 1984 he was admitted to practice in the State of Florida and admitted before the U.S. Tax Court and the 11th Circuit Court of Appeals. Mr. Paleveda became a partner in the tax law firm Hampton, Paleveda, Murphy, Cody and Levy which employed 13 J.D. LL.M or J.D. CPA tax attorneys in Florida. In 1989 Mr. Paleveda went to work for Mutual Benefit Life. While at Mutual Benefit Life, Mr. Paleveda conducted over 1,000 Advanced Tax and Estate Planning Seminars throughout the U.S. in almost every major city until 1993. In 1997, he became a contributing author for "The Life Insurance Answer Book for Qualified Plans and Estate Planning" published by Panel Publishing now a division of ASPEN publishing and taught Retirement Planning for the College for Financial Planning at Oglethorpe University in Atlanta. In 2001, Mr. Paleveda became President of a TPA firm in Seattle. In 2006, Mr. Paleveda became the CEO of Executive Benefits Design Group in Bellingham Washington. Mr. Paleveda is married with two children. His hobbies are chess and trivia. He was ranked No. 10 among high school chess players. Mr. Paleveda was a USCF Chess Master and the Florida State Chess Champion in 1977, 1978, and 1994.

Below are Marjorie, Nick (A.) and grandhild Caelen , our greatest achievement to date, and who, along with his parents, uncle, and siblings and cousins to come (Nick E. are you paying attention?) will be our greatest and most enduring legacies.